The John Birch Society

The John Birch Society

Anatomy of a Protest

by

J. ALLEN BROYLES

With a new concluding chapter

BEACON PRESS   BOSTON

To Dolores

Author's Note

This study of the John Birch Society was begun in February, 1961, but the major emphasis has been upon interviews (which included the use of a questionnaire) with leaders, members, and opponents of the Birch Society in Massachusetts, Kansas, Arkansas, Texas, Arizona, and California made in the Spring of 1962. Additional interviews have been conducted since then in Massachusetts, New York City, and Washington, D.C., to keep abreast of the changes within the Society. In these interviews, the author never sought to identify himself as a "convert" to the Birch Society, but always clearly identified himself as a graduate student doing research. In reporting these interviews, the names have been changed except for those who had been publicly identified as members of the John Birch Society at the time of the interview, or who were publicly affiliated with the Society at the time that this book went to press.

The John Birch Society: Anatomy of a Protest is a revision of a doctoral dissertation submitted to the Department of Sociology and Social Ethics of the Graduate School, Boston University, in 1963. Grateful acknowledgment is here made to Professor Paul Deats, Dean Walter Muelder, and Professor Robert Chin for their guidance and criticism of that study. Since completing residence and field research for the doctoral dissertation in June, 1962, the author has served as pastor of the First Methodist Church of Boothbay Harbor, Maine. Grateful acknowledgment is made of the patience of that congregation with the demands of scholarship and authorship which have been made upon their pastor. Thanks is also expressed to Miss Virginia Ross, who undertook the task of typing handwritten manuscript for the dissertation and for this book. Albert V. Danielson was gracious enough to contribute funds for the expenses involved in typing. My debt to a great many others all across this country who have shared their observations and insights about the Birch Society locally and nationally is much too extensive either to be catalogued or ever to be fully repaid.

J.A.B.

Boothbay Harbor, Maine
March, 1964

Contents

Introduction

The home of the John Birch Society is in a quiet old suburb of Boston and consequently Belmont 78 (now Belmont, Massachusetts, 02178) is the source of the stream of comment from Robert H. W. Welch, Jr., mailed out under the return address of *American Opinion.* Every letter and package bears on its metered postage sticker the admonition: "This is a republic, not a democracy— Let's keep it that way!" The message is cryptic and I approached this bastion of our republic with awe and curiosity.

"AMERICAN OPINION" says the sign on the home office, this temple of an all-too-articulate latter-day Oracle of Delphi, appropriately set beside a quiet, tree-lined street not far from "the hub of the universe." The building's walls are of neat red brick; its windows, surprisingly enough, are of clear, clean glass, distorted only by the narrow slats of Venetian blinds. Shared with a prominent insurance company, the "temple" appears to be divided evenly between them, but fittingly enough, for an organization often described as semi-secret, the Birch Society uses the first floor and entire basement of this and an adjacent building, the top floor of which is occupied by another insurance company. The very housing of its offices symbolize secrecy—one-fifth visible and four-fifths submerged. On the other side of these offices is the Belmont Branch of the United States Post Office, and the John Birch Society is probably its biggest customer.

As I neared the front door of *American Opinion,* I carefully examined every pedestrian, eying suspiciously even a neatly dressed, middle-aged man coming down the street toward me. Each of us was probably wondering: Is he a member . . . or an administrator . . . or a co-ordinator? We passed each other and he mumbled in response to my mumbled greeting. He entered the office of the insurance company next door and I, perhaps confirming his suspicions, went toward the door marked *American Opinion.*

Noting a parking space reserved for Robert Welch, I also found that there was something the matter with the double door at the entrance. One side was locked and I had to "pull" when it said "push," but I collected my wits and finally negotiated an entrance of sorts into a narrow hallway. There was a stairway to the right with a sketch of John Birch prominently displayed halfway down, and signs directed one along the hall through a door to the left. As I entered I found myself standing in front of a switchboard in a large office with five or six desks. Two men and the three or four women looked up appraisingly. I apparently passed the test, for one of the young men came forward to greet me. I introduced myself and said that I wanted to find out about the John Birch Society. He offered to take me on a tour, and two other people appeared behind me—a couple in their late thirties—members of the Society from California.

The tour began right there. The young man pointed out Mr. Welch's adjoining office in the front of the building. And, since Mr. Welch was out, we all peered in at the spacious but rather ordinary-looking room with a desk in the far corner and a few chairs. The long inside wall is completely lined with books and pamphlets; many of them appeared to be the blue-and-white-backed copies of the regular monthly *American Opinion.*

American Opinion is the successor to *One Man's Opinion,* which Welch began to edit and publish in 1956. Issued somewhat irregularly in only a few thousand copies per issue, the title of *One Man's Opinion* was changed to *American Opinion* in 1958 when the John Birch Society was founded. According to the December, 1963, statement of ownership, management, and circulation, it is published monthly except July, the average number of issues distributed is 27,060—to subscribers 15,453 and to agents and news dealers 10,858. The remainder were distributed through miscellaneous channels. Up to January, 1964, it averaged 80 pages and its price was fifty cents per issue. Since then it has been expanded to 100 pages with a price per issue of one dollar. It consists largely of articles on past and current history, documenting, to their authors' and Welch's satisfaction, the nature and progress of the "Communist conspiracy."

As we surveyed Mr. Welch's office, the lady from California

supplied all the "Oh's" and "Ah's" necessary. We were introduced to the switchboard operator and to two or three of the rest of the staff. They nodded back in vacant frozen-smiled public-relations fashion and returned to their work.

From this first-floor office we were led back through the narrow hall and down the stairs, passing under the sketch of John Birch. The downstairs office area spreads across the entire basement of the building. One corner on the left is blocked off by file cabinets and partitions and our genial guide identified it as the research department. There appeared to be about thirty desks in the entire basement and our guide proceeded to point out the other departments. It seems that all the incoming mail is processed and most of it either filed or answered right there. Some of it requires the personal attention of Mr. Welch, and some of it is referred to other departments, but most of it can be handled by this department of about twenty people. The other department, in the far right-hand corner from the stairway, handles the directing of the approximately forty field co-ordinators, who organize and direct local chapters of the Society across the country.

We were ushered over to meet a man in his early thirties with black, thinning hair; he was somewhat portly and dressed in a dark suit. He apparently heads the department and his visage bore the scowl-squint of high dedication. On the wall behind his desk was a large map of our United States, sprinkled or riddled with pins which designated chapters, bookstores, and co-ordinators. The pins were most heavily concentrated in several cities in Texas and Southern California. But there were other significant concentrations in Phoenix, Wichita, and along the North Shore of Chicago. There appeared to be no state without a pin of some sort.

With the lady from California continuing to "Oh," and "Ah," in barely subdued squeals and shrieks, we proceeded to an exit at the left-rear corner of the basement, up a flight of stairs, out into daylight, across the asphalt parking lot to the adjacent business and editorial offices of the magazine, *American Opinion*. We met the editor and the business manager, both personable young men.

From these fairly small offices we were taken to the mailing room. The stock men and clerks were getting the latest monthly *Bulletin* ready for mailing. Not being well schooled in middle-class mores, they just looked up blankly and made no response to our smiles. But this rebuff was softened. We were all given advance copies of the *Bulletin*. The lady from California was almost overcome by her good fortune.

We retraced our steps to the basement of the main building. There the tour was lifted to an unexpected climax! At the foot of the stairs, under the framed sketch of John Birch, we met Robert Welch, the Founder. All of us had seen his likeness at one time or another in newspapers, but face to face! The lady from California contained herself only with extreme effort, realizing that proper decorum called for some vestige of restraint. Standing before us was a man in his early sixties, of medium slightly paunchy stature, with a balding head. Excitable, somewhat nervous and jumpy in manner, he was in shirtsleeves and in need of a shave. One of the ladies at a nearby desk told us in a stage whisper that he had been up all night! Working!

Our guide, Mr. McKinney, who remembered our names, pronunciation and all, introduced us each in turn to Mr. Welch. All of us shook hands, smiled and made some comment reasonably appropriate to this occasion. The lady from California undoubtedly found her mood shifting from manic to depressive all the way home as she and her husband relived this high moment and she wished she had had something *really* appropriate to say or ask— but she didn't.

The tour was complete; anything else would have been anti-climactic. Recognizing this, we thanked our guide, shook hands, exchanged smiles and "thank yous" all around and parted in a mood already become reflective. Impressions, reactions, and questions filled our minds. The California couple left in a state not unlike that of persons leaving a very meaningful service of worship. But for one who is not a member of the John Birch Society, questions pushed forward. I had been received with courtesy and had met a number of people, including the guide, who were polished in the arts of public relations which, even to a critical observer, bordered at times upon genuine friendliness and interest.

Yet the questions persist. What is the purpose, what is the meaning of such an organization upon our American scene?

CHAPTER I

The Golden Past
and Tarnished Present

"We're here to save our Country from a *Communistic plot*," runs a line from the satirical song, "The John Birch Society," done by the Chad Mitchell Trio. And the line is correct. Members of the Birch Society do believe that collapse of our country is imminent. They believe, moreover, that this collapse was blueprinted by Lenin at the time of the Russian revolution and is about to be precipitated by a vast web of Communistic subversives who hold high places in all walks of our national life. We're the most powerful nation on earth, yet we're losing to the Communists. Subversion must be the answer, they reason.

Dark warnings of imminent collapse and cries of subversion are nothing new upon the American scene. We have never lacked a self-appointed "second line of defense" behind our duly constituted watchmen and guardians. It seems to grow in numbers and its voice to swell in volume during times of crisis.

The usual "solution" for all crisis, by the right wing of this "second line of defense," is a return to the "pure" and "fundamental" economic, political, and religious beliefs, values, and institutional forms of a distant past—a distant past, embellished and blurred by the rosy haze of memory and myth. The actual problems and alternatives which our duly constituted leaders face are ignored. The unrealistic exhortations to return to the "pure fundamentals," accompanied by attacks upon leaders who do not share these views, provide little more than the luxury of escape.

The Birch Society has a great deal in common with the irrealism and escape of other movements of social protest during or following a time of crisis. Irrealism and escape are certainly apparent in the extremely unsystematic "program" of the Society for the eradication of what it sees as communism, and its even more unsystematic attempts to revive the "pure" and "fundamental" beliefs, values, and institutional forms of economics, politics, and religion drawn from the distant past.

The era in which we live is truly one of crisis and bewildering change, but our situation is seen by the John Birch Society as one all-pervasive illness, with only one suitable remedy. The crisis is seen as the Armageddon, the final battle, between individualism and collectivism. The illness is the disease of collectivism, inevitably leading to communism. The one suitable remedy, as the Society sees it, is to root out all thought and leadership to the left of a distorted "protectionist" Adam Smith in economics, Barry Goldwater in politics, Carl McIntire in religion, and the "three R's" in education.

The Birch Society hopes for the day when they will see "really" patriotic economics, patriotic politics, patriotic religion, and patriotic education. The leaders and members of the Society have no doubt that their ideas are the only ones that are "really" patriotic, and they regard all who differ with them as conscious or unconscious agents of an international Communist conspiracy. The agonized plea goes out: "Save our country from communism, communism in all its hidden forms. Help us destroy this menace, and we can all go back to a normal life."

The emphasis on one problem is familiar. "Get rid of alien Romanism," whispered the "Know Nothings." "Free the slaves," shouted the Abolitionists. "Keep the Negro in his place," echoed the KKK. "Give *us* the vote and end corruption," chanted the Suffragettes. And "stop the flow of demon rum," added the Prohibitionists.

One problem is made the keystone of every ill of society. Dislodge it, and all the other problems tumble, too. The call is clear. The response of the naïve has often been overwhelming.

The whisper and the cry are once again abroad in our land, the whisper insinuating that our most trusted leaders have betrayed us all. And the cry or the whisper alone have provided past movements with enough support to enable them to wield great power. Will the John Birch Society achieve a similar place in our history?

The John Birch Society was founded in 1958, when Robert Welch invited eleven men, most of them older businessmen, to Indianapolis to consider the direction he felt the country was taking. Some of these men had already been introduced to his fairly standard right-wing views through their reading of his magazine *One Man's Opinion* and his controversial "private letter," *The Politician*. During a two-day session, December eighth and ninth, Welch presented his analysis of the sad state of the union and proposed the formation of the John Birch Society as the remedy. The transcript of this two-day marathon presentation was published as the *Blue Book*, the "bible of the Society." These men agreed that the proposed John Birch Society, under Welch's leadership, might be capable of halting and reversing what they believed to be disastrous and Communistically manipulated economic and political trends.

Before we turn to a consideration of the leader and the organization of the Birch Society, we need to examine its most important documents, *The Politician*[1] and the *Blue Book*.[2]

The Politician has stirred up a great deal of controversy primarily because of Welch's conclusion about Dwight D. Eisenhower. What Welch wrote in an early version was: "My firm belief that Dwight Eisenhower is a dedicated, conscious agent of the Communist conspiracy is based on an accumulation of detailed evidence so extensive and so palpable that it seems to me to put this conviction beyond any reasonable doubt."[3] The phrase describing Eisenhower as "a conscious agent of the Communist conspiracy" has been thrown back at Robert Welch so often that in the current edition of *The Politician* he chose to omit this statement and its three surrounding paragraphs.

But even in the current edition the author says: "The suggestion cannot be ignored that Eisenhower's motivation has been more ideologically honest than shallowly opportunistic. Or, to put the matter bluntly, he has been sympathetic to ultimate Communist aims, realistically and even mercilessly willing to help them achieve their goals, knowingly receiving and abiding by Communist orders, and consciously serving the Communist conspiracy for all his adult life."[4]

But Welch does grant one major alternative to this view of

Eisenhower as a Communist conspirator. It is phrased as a rhetorical question. "Could Eisenhower really be simply a smart politician, entirely without principles and hungry for glory, who is only the tool of the Communists?"[5] The affirmative answer gave to Welch's book its title: *The Politician*.

The involved story of *The Politician* had an interesting beginning. In December, 1954, in a car proceeding toward New York City, four men were in earnest conversation. The topic of the latest election was brought up by one of them. Robert Welch expressed the view that President Eisenhower had double-crossed a number of conservative candidates for the House and the Senate by failing to help them out in their campaigns after having promised to do so. These candidates had counted heavily on Eisenhower to campaign in their behalf—but, Welch went on, Eisenhower put them off with one excuse after another. Welch added that, in his opinion, this double-cross by Eisenhower was intentional. One of the other three men was so appalled at this suggestion that he asked why Eisenhower would do this intentionally. Welch expounded on aspects of Eisenhower's background that led him to this conclusion. The questioner was still in doubt and he asked for a written account of these views so that he could study them more thoroughly. This was agreeable and from this request, *The Politician* had its birth. Robert Welch sent carbon copies of these early notes to his other two friends as well. One or two of these men requested additional copies of this material to send to still other friends.

Requests continued to come in and Robert Welch continued to expand on his views of Eisenhower until, within three years, the material had grown to two hundred pages and was being reproduced by offset printing and bound in a plastic binding with black covers. Welch says he distributed *The Politician* or the *Black Book* to trusted friends and their acquaintances, but apparently *The Politician* received somewhat wider circulation.

On July 26, 1960, when *The Politician* was nearly six years old and the Birch Society nearly two, there was the first "exposure" of *The Politician* by Jack Mabley of the *Chicago Daily News*. On January 22 and 23, 1961, Hans Engh, a staff writer for the Santa Barbara *News-Press,* did two articles on the Birch Society in response to the appearance of local chapters in Santa Barbara. On February 26, 1961, Thomas M. Storke, editor and publisher of the *News-Press* ran a scathing editorial on the Birch Society. Mr. Storke prefaced his editorial with a personal comment: "The editor and publisher of the *News-Press* is in his eighty-fifth year. His entire life has been spent in this community. His memory takes him back many years and his reading even further. He lived when conditions were rugged. When the West was West and men were men. He lived during periods when if a man or group of men openly by word of mouth, or the printed word, called our president, our vice president, our secretary of state, the president's brother, members of the Supreme Court, and others at the head of our government, traitors, they were made to answer. Such slanders often called for a visit from a courageous and irate group which brought with them a barrel of tar and a few feathers. And such instances were particularly likely to occur if the slanderer came from New England. He lived when men were considered cowards when they hid behind women's skirts and clothed their identity through anonymity."

One day earlier, February 25, an article on the Birch Society had appeared in the *People's World*, a newspaper of the far left, in San Francisco. A few days later, on April 10, *Time* magazine also ran an article on the Society. In all of these articles a prominent place was given to Welch's allegations about Eisenhower in *The Politician*.

Robert Welch reacted to this public exposure of *The Politician* in a number of ways. First of all, he built up a rather elaborate case about this "Communistically inspired smear" on the Birch Society, dating it from what he described as the "mother article" in the *People's World*.[6] This theory has one rather large hole in it. Jack Mabley's column in the Chicago *Daily News* appeared six months earlier, and Hans Engh's two articles in the Santa Barbara *News-Press* appeared more than a month earlier than this alleged "mother article" in the *People's World*.

Welch felt that the campaign to smear the Birch Society because of his allegations about Eisenhower was "viciously unfair" for several reasons. First of all, he explains, the founders of the Society disavowed *The Politician* in 1958 and "the Council of the

Society long ago officially made it clear that this was a purely personal property and problem of my own, with which they wanted nothing whatsoever to do in any way."[7] "Not only ... was this manuscript no part of the beliefs or materials of the Society, but most of the members had never even heard of it before being blamed for what it said. They were being accused of something for which they had taken no responsibility whatsoever. Although I myself was perfectly willing to take the responsibility for whatever I had written, there was simply no way that I could defend myself or my statements without publishing the whole document of which these statements were a part. This the Leftists gambled, correctly, I would be unwilling to do; not because of any possible further damage to myself, but because of probable damage to the whole Conservative cause, through trying to lead people too rapidly into a realization of truths that they were unwilling to accept."[8]

Another response that Welch made to this "smear" was to issue an official statement from the Belmont home office. This statement read in part: "Nowhere in my private or published writings have I ever called former President Eisenhower a 'card-carrying' Communist. Anybody who says I have is either knowingly dealing in falsehoods or is badly misinformed."[9] In response to the charge that he had accused Eisenhower of being a "conscious agent of the Communist conspiracy," this oft-repeated "defense" by Mr. Welch is somewhat less than forthright.

Since the controversy over his charge about Eisenhower refused to die down, Welch finally decided to alter *The Politician* somewhat and publish it. "For a number of reasons . . . I have at last decided to give to friends of mine, and to anybody else—friend or enemy—who really cares, an opportunity to read this manuscript *now, as is,* so that they can judge it for themselves. In doing so they may gain a better understanding of much that is happening today, through seeing current developments as merely an extension or completion of actions taken and trends initiated during the [Eisenhower] Administration. And if the Liberals do not like this result of their unceasing and utterly unfair attacks, they have only themselves to blame. Any man, hounded long enough and mercilessly enough, for merely saying what he believes and doing what he thinks is right, is entitled at long last to defend himself."[10]

In *The Politician* any personal or political contacts or friendships with national or international figures of whom Barry Goldwater, Carl McIntire, Adam Smith, or Robert Welch would not approve—any military or foreign policy negotiations with our World War II ally and our Cold War enemy Russia, any international losses to communism, and *especially* any negotiated mutual concessions—*all together* make up Welch's "case" which "documents" the "use" of Eisenhower by the Communists.

Welch would say that *The Politician* leaves its reader with only two choices: That Eisenhower was (1) an "unconscious" or (2) a "conscious" agent of the Communist conspiracy. Let me suggest a third possibility—that Welch and his followers are so naïve that they are unable to distinguish possibility, rumor, and falsehood from fact; nebulous inference, paranoid suspicion, and specious argument from sound conclusion. And finally, they are so naïve as to seem unable to conclude that domestic or international political and economic grievance or disappointment can come from the hands of any but a traitorous leader.

The Blue Book

The Politician is interesting because of what it reveals about what and how the founder of the Birch Society thinks. And it has assumed considerably more importance now that it has been published and is available to members and non-members alike. But *The Politician* is not the Society's basic document. The *Blue Book,* the edited transcript of Welch's two-day speech at the "founding" of the Society, is the basic document.

The *Blue Book* has always been much less mysterious than *The Politician* simply because it has long been available to anyone who might wish to obtain it through the Belmont home office. Much of its content, however, is fully as inflammatory as that of *The Politician*. A number of quotes from the *Blue Book* throughout this study of the Society will substantiate this assertion, but one quote here will serve as an illustration. Speaking of the grad-

ual subversive takeover of the United States government by the
Communists, which Welch asserted in 1958 was "going on right
now," he envisioned the time when the American people "can no
longer resist the Communist conspiracy as free citizens, but can
resist the Communist tyranny only by themselves becoming conspirators against established government."[11]

As recorded in the *Blue Book,* the major divisions of Welch's
presentation in Indianapolis string together into some sort of
"story." They are: "Look at the Score—But Let's Look Deeper—
And Deeper Still—And So, Let's Act—Under Positive Leadership
—To Restore Responsibility—And Help to Build a Better World
—Through The John Birch Society." As with much other material
from the pen of Robert Welch, the logic and coherence is more apparent than real. Let us look at some of the highlights of this speech
which, as we have seen, lasted through most of two days:

"Look at the Score"

Mr. Welch begins with the thesis that the Communists
have been successful and on schedule in their move toward world
domination. He cites their plan as that of Lenin, a plan which
the Russian leader never stated, but which has become nevertheless a very popular quote of the American right wing. The "paraphrase" and "summary" of Lenin's plan is as follows: "First we
will take Eastern Europe. Next, the mass of Asia. Then we shall
encircle that last bastion of capitalism, the United States of
America. We shall not have to attack; it will fall like overripe
fruit into our hands."[12] Welch maintains that the Communists have
been successful in the first two steps and that they are very near
success in the last. This final step—the infiltration and subversion
of the United States—he sees as taking place in the piecemeal
surrender of sovereignty to the UN and other international agencies and in the transformation of the United States into a Socialist
nation which could be "comfortably merged with Soviet Russia."
According to Welch, the Communists ". . . have let nothing
stand in their way, and nothing divert them. They have used the
philosophy of socialism as an ideological weapon, in this struggle,
whenever they could and for whatever it was worth. But it was

only one of their many weapons. They have also used bribery, lies, bluff, brutality, the countless tentacles of treason, murder on a scale never before dreamed of in the world, and every possible means to advance them on this road, without the slightest concern for any moral difference in those various means. And above all, they have used patience. *A patient gradualism has been the most important key to the Communists' overwhelming success.*"[13]

Welch maintains that "this is a *world-wide* battle, the first in history, between light and darkness; between freedom and slavery; between the spirit of Christianity and the spirit of anti-Christ in the souls and bodies of men."[14] He concludes this apocalyptic analysis with the exhortation: ". . . let's win that battle by alertness, by determination, by courage, by an energizing realization of the danger, if we can; but let's win it even with our lives if the time comes when we must."[15]

"But Let's Look Deeper"

Mr. Welch's next assertion is that of Spengler's *Decline of the West:* that the growth of individualism is parallel to the growth of civilization, and that the growth of collectivism is parallel to its decay. Welch sees communism as simply the most obvious current symptom of the "cancer" of collectivism.

Welch draws an analogy between "individual" and "social" disease which is rather doubtful both medically and sociologically. He states that "An individual human being may die of any number of causes. But if he escapes the fortuitous diseases, does not meet with any fatal accident, does not starve to death, does not have his heart give out, but lives in normal health to his three score years and ten and then keeps on living—if he escapes and keeps on doing so, he will eventually succumb to the degenerative disease of cancer. For death must come, and cancer is merely death coming by stages, instead of all at once. And exactly the same thing seems to be true of those organic aggregations of human beings, which we call cultures or civilizations."[16] Thus, according to him, we must not only destroy communism, we must also destroy all other manifestations of the more basic "disease" of collectivism.

"And Deeper Still"

Welch goes on to say that the loss of fundamentalist religious faith represents the decay of our civilization at an even deeper level. He thinks that he has a common religious ground for all his followers "without any of us doing the slightest violation to the more specific doctrines of his own creed or altars of his own devotion . . . an ennobling conception, equally acceptable to the most fundamentalist Christian or the most rationalistic idealist . . . a conception which the Baptist John Birch, the Catholic Hilaire Belloc, and the agnostic Thomas Jefferson would alike have welcomed."[17] Welch promises to provide this common, religious ground later in the *Blue Book,* but he says that the failure to find a meaningful religious base has brought about the rise of "amoral man."

In an apparent reference to John Kennedy, Welch had this to say in December 1958: "Among the millions who either are, or pretend to be, non-Communists, the amoral man, who has no slightest inner concern with right or wrong, is one of the greatest causes of our constant retreat, and one of the greatest dangers to our survival. And he doesn't wear any label. He usually lives up to the appearance of excellent morals, because it is expedient for his purposes, and you will usually find him in church on Sunday morning, maybe even a Catholic church. But as a member of the United States Senate, running for the presidency, and smart enough to know the strong Communist support behind-the-scenes which he will have to get in order to have any chance of being nominated in 1960, such an amoral man can do a tremendous amount of ball-carrying on behalf of Communist aims here in the United States . . . And any similarity of characters in this story to any living persons is not coincidental."[18]

"And So, Let's Act"

The problems of Western civilization having been thus "exposed," Welch says that the place to begin to act is in the United States, for two reasons. "First, because it must be our more earnest hope and goal to break out of this straightjacket [sic] woven of pretense, deception, audacity, and terror, before it completely encompasses ourselves. And second, because the American support of the Communist conspiracy is now the backbone of its strength, and has been for many years. If and when we can reach the point of turning just the American government from actively helping the Communist conspiracy everywhere in the world, we shall have won a most important battle in the war ahead."[19]

The need, as Welch sees it, is to generate public pressure that will reverse what he perceives as Communistic trends within our government. He proposes the following measures to create this public pressure under his leadership as "the man on the white horse:"

1. He would establish reading rooms with "properly" Americanist books and periodicals in as many cities and towns as possible.

2. He would have these reading rooms and his followers extend the circulation of Americanist periodicals—especially *American Opinion.*

3. He would urge that his followers support and widen the stations and the audiences for the radio programs of Fulton Lewis, Clarence Manion, and others.

4. He would organize and control a co-ordinated program of letter-writing.

5. He would urge his followers to "organize fronts—little fronts, big fronts, permanent fronts, all kinds of fronts."[20] He lauded the "Committee of One Million" in its efforts to keep Red China out of the UN. He suggested as other new possibilities "A Petition to Impeach Earl Warren," "A Committee to Investigate Communist Influences at Vassar College," "Women Against Labor Union Hoodlumism," and others.

6. "Another thing we should do, and one badly needed, would be to start shocking the American people . . . into a realization of what is happening. . . . The best way to do this is by exposure, which is why the Communists just had to get rid of McCarthy, and went to such extreme lengths to do so."[21]

Upon identifying a suspected Communist, "we would run in the magazine an article consisting entirely of questions to this man, which would be devastating in their implications. The question technique when skillfully used in this way is mean and dirty. But the Communists we are after are meaner and dirtier, and too slippery for you to put your fingers on them in the ordinary way. . . ."[22] Welch warns darkly that "one of the hardest things for the ordinary decent American to realize is that a secret Communist looks and acts just like anybody else, only more so; or that anybody he, the ordinary decent American, happens to know personally, could possibly be a Communist."[23] As one can see, the task of hating Communists can get very complex—and a good many of the followers of Welch take the easy way out and just hate everybody except their friends—whom they only suspect.

7.   Robert Welch's seventh point is a tirade against Gordon Hall, a well-known lecturer and writer on extremist groups of both the right and the left. It seems that, as early as 1958—before the Birch Society was even formed, Gordon Hall had identified Robert Welch as an extremist of the right. Welch suggests that questioners harass Gordon Hall whenever he speaks, in an attempt to "expose" him.

8.   He would line up a huge list of "Americanist" speakers who would be willing to speak to small church groups, PTA groups, or similar organizations for little or no fee.

9.   He would urge his followers to start extending their efforts to other countries and begin to undertake activities on the international front as soon as possible.

10.   Finally he would urge them to exert their influence in political campaigns as quickly as possible. He cites the "Committee on Political Organization" (COPE), of the AFL-CIO as one worthy of emulation in its modus operandi if not in its goals. Robert Welch, in this and other instances, seems to picture himself as the right-wing or conservative counterpart of Walter Reuther.

Welch concluded this portion (addressed originally to his eleven weary auditors on December 8, 1958), by commenting that "we are in circumstances where it is *realistic* to be *fantastic*."[24] Following this enigmatic observation, he allowed them to have some supper and go to bed.

"Under Positive Leadership"

First thing in the morning of December 9, these eleven auditors apparently gathered for one more solid day of Welch's marathon speech. We shall examine what he said when we consider Welch's concept of leadership, but the identity of the leader in question should not be difficult for anyone to guess.

"I want to convince you," Robert Welch told his eleven listeners, "as I am convinced, that only dynamic *personal* leadership offers any chance for us to save either our material or our spiritual inheritance. I want to convince you, as I am convinced, that even under such leadership we have no chance unless the specific battles are fought *as a part of a larger and more lasting movement to restore once again an upward reach to the heart of man,* and I have wished to make clear, what you were bound to be assuming already, that whatever I have in me, of faith, dedication, and energy, I intend to offer that leadership to all who are willing to help me."[25]

"To Restore Responsibility"

What is to be the task of this leadership? Quickly stated, its aim is to promote "less government and more responsibility." Welch goes into an extended ten-point discourse on government, concluding with the contention that "neither the form of government nor its quality is as important as its quantity . . . " that "The increasing quantity of government, in all nations, has constituted the greatest tragedy of the Twentieth Century."[26]

He then gives his definitions of theoretical "communism" and "Americanism." "The Communist believes that a collectivist society should swallow up all individuals, make their lives and their energies completely subservient to the needs and the purposes of the collectivist state; and that any means are permissible to that end. The true *americanist* believes that the individual should retain the freedom to make his own bargain with life, and the responsibility for the results of that bargain; and that the means are as important as the ends in the civilized social order which he desires."[27]

I have no argument with these definitions of what are essentially totalitarian and democratic governments, but Welch falters repeatedly at the point of the means to achieve a democratic society. He grants that the "means are as important as ends," but his concept of the structure of the Birch Society which is to be its means to achieve the goal of an Americanist government is, as we shall see, clearly totalitarian. One could define the functioning of the Birch Society in the same terms that Welch uses to define communism: "The follower of Welch believes that the John Birch Society should swallow up individuals, make their lives and energies completely subservient to the needs and the purposes of the Birch Society under the leadership of Welch; and that any means are permissible to achieve the end of a 'truly Americanist' government—the definition of which is left to their leader." Welch actually has many more ideas about what constitutes "true Americanism" then he gives in his definition. He also says that "there are many stages of welfarism, socialism, and collectivism in general, but communism is the ultimate state of them all, and they all lead inevitably in that direction."[28] The more Welch elaborates, the less clear his definitions become. But, within a political context, the line he draws between Americanism and communism would seem to be between Taft and Eisenhower in 1952 and between Goldwater and Nixon in 1964. This line of demarcation would identify more than three-fourths of the body politic as Communist agents or dupes. It's no wonder that members of the Birch Society tend to be somewhat clannish and suspicious!

"And Help to Build a Better World"

Welch now returns to his promised religious synthesis—a "bedrock of faith"—which is to undergird the new morality and unite the members of the John Birch Society. And here he shows his talent in the use of metaphor: this bedrock of faith has two keystones. The "first keystone" is a doctrine of God. Welch maintains that it is best expressed in the words of Tennyson: "For I doubt not through the ages one increasing purpose runs." Welch apparently sees some purpose from some source apart from the disintegration and decay of civilization that has preoccupied him up to this point in this report. But both the purpose and its source are unidentified.

This brings us to the "second keystone," a doctrine of man, which Welch delineates in the words of another poet, one Harry Kemp: "Thou hast put an upward reach in the heart of man." Though this doctrine is mentioned as the second, it actually is the primary keystone of Welch's bedrock of faith. It seems to him "that, to make us truly religious, we do not need to know anything more about God, man, and man's relationship to God than is given by a reverent understanding of that line."[29] Apparently Welch sees his mission as Messianic—to tell to all of us precisely what that "one increasing purpose" is, and to direct our "reach" in the direction that is truly "upward." That appears to be quite an undertaking for any mortal unaided by any scripture beyond ambiguous poetry, but Robert Welch seems a willing volunteer.

There they are—the two keystones of a bedrock of faith—a "faith" which "unites" all faiths by blurring any authentic and meaningful affirmations to which they have come, a "faith" which finds content only at the convenience of its founder and only as his purposes dictate. But I digress. Hear the comforting words as Robert Welch asks reassuringly, ". . . what firmer foundation can we possibly need for the faith on which to build our new age and with which to inaugurate the dream that is coming to birth"[30]

Through The John Birch Society

Welch believes that his dynamic personal leadership can best be expressed through an authoritarian organizational structure. He says that in order to withstand ". . . the stresses and strains of internal difference and external animosities, throughout changing political climates over long periods of time; for the building of morale and loyalty and a feeling of unified purpose and closely knit strength; for effective functioning in periods of crisis and a permanence of high dedication throughout more peaceful decades; for these and many other reasons *The John Birch Society will operate under completely authoritative control at all levels.* The fear of tyrannical oppression of individuals, and other arguments against the authoritative structure in the form of governments, have little bearing on the case of a voluntary association, where the authoritative power can be exercised and enforced only by persuasion. And what little validity they do have is outweighed by the advantages of firm and positive direction of the Society's energies. Especially for the near future, and for the fight against Communism which is the first great task of the Society, it is imperative that all the strength we can muster be subject to smoothly functioning direction from the top. As I have said before, no collection of debating societies is ever going to stop the Communist conspiracy from taking us over, and I have no intention of adding another frustrated group to their number. We mean business every step of the way."[31]

But what of its purpose? "Our short-range purpose, our long-range purpose, and our lasting purpose, is to promote less government, more responsibility, and a better world. That says it all. It is, I think, simple, understandable, and all-inclusive as to the goals for which we strive."[32] It seems clear that this purpose, like the bedrock of faith upon which it is reared, is wide open to any content and direction its leader may choose to give it.

As he prepared to undertake leadership of this venture, Welch said: "It is my fervent hope that the John Birch Society will last for hundreds of years, and exert an increasing influence for the temporal good and the spiritual ennoblement of mankind throughout those centuries. For I am staking my whole aspiration to play my part, in forwarding man's one increasing purpose, on whatever can be accomplished through the John Birth Society. I want no other title than that of its Founder, and I have no other ambition for anything resembling fame or historical remembrance."[33]

The two-day meeting in Indianapolis drew to a close. The eleven men had been presented with a program and a leader to take care of the spiritual and cultural decay of which communism was only a symptom. It is, indeed, unfortunate that the transcript of the meeting breaks off at that point. How, precisely, was the

John Birch Society founded? By a rising ovation to its leader? By a secret ballot? By the absence of any dissent? The act of "founding" is shrouded in mystery. We know only that nine of the eleven men did consent to become members of the Council. One more consented at a later date. But all of them, who had not yet read the packets of material given them by Welch, must have wondered about the name of the Society. Why John Birch?

CHAPTER II

The Upstaged Hero

The scene shifts. The time is 1952, at the height of the McCarthy era. The place is a room in the Senate Office Building in our nation's capital. An independent investigator sits alone poring over the vast literature of Congressional hearings related to the Communist menace at home and abroad—page after page of fine print, a verbatim of questions and answers, which would appall any grade-school teacher of English. Liberally sprinkled with the "documentation" of articles and affidavits, such hearings are usually prefaced with a statement, often ignored, to the effect that "this testimony is not evaluated and no inference of subversive affiliation or activity should be made solely because the name of a person, organization, or publication is mentioned in the report." But such hearings are read and republished ("not at governmental expense") by the American right wing as gospel truth.

Seated at a table with page after page and volume after volume passing beneath his careful scrutiny, the citizen investigator suddenly stops. Before him is "evidence" of the duplicity of our governmental leaders—in the army! His suspicions are further deepened since the report was only typewritten and never published! He reads on. From what he can gather from this fragmentary report, there has been a conscious attempt to bury the first casualty of "World War III" in obscurity rather than in glory. Robert Welch has found John Birch and sees his duty clearly. Americans must be told the hushed-up story of their unknown hero son, John Birch. Welch visits the parents of John Birch on their tree farm near Macon, Georgia. He continues for over a year to gather accounts of John's life and of the circumstances of his death. In 1954, four years before the founding of the John Birch Society, Robert Welch's *The Life of John Birch* is published.[1]

According to Welch's biography, John Birch was born

May 18, 1918, in India where his parents were serving as missionaries. Although Methodists, they were in India under the auspices of the Presbyterian Church, U.S.A., and they have since moved to a more fundamentalist position and have come to describe themselves as "Bible believing" Baptists. In India, John's father taught vocational agriculture and his mother taught English. When his father's health broke, the family had to return to the United States. For a time they settled in his mother's home town of Vineland, New Jersey, and then returned to the old and run-down family farm in Georgia. The depression was very difficult for the Birches, but they did manage to provide an education for their seven children. John, the eldest, and the other children were given a strongly fundamentalist Christian training by their parents. John graduated at the head of his high-school class and went on to college at nearby Southern Baptist Mercer. One of his classmates remembers John at Mercer University as:

. . . one of the most brilliant fellows I've ever met. He made A's almost automatically. He was a wizard not only in making grades but in many practical fields and could do almost anything to which he set his mind.

John was also one of the most dynamic personalities I ever knew. He had a personal magnetism, was a born leader, and was capable and gifted without measure.

One of his great traits was deep conviction and evangelistic passion. When he believed a thing he was absolutely unbending. He had a will of his own like few persons I ever met.

It was at the point of convictions that John and I parted ways, though it did not mar our personal relationship. John was convinced several professors at Mercer were teaching heresy. Along with twelve other ministerial students, he circulated charges of heresy against the professors, including my revered teacher in the religion department. A heresy hearing resulted in which John was one of the star witnesses against the teachers. The teachers were exonerated of the charges, but the religion professor I revered so highly never overcame the mortal wounds of the affair.

I sat through the heresy hearing. I heard the statements used by John against the religion professor. I had been in the same class. I thought the charges were untrue and unfair and still do, though I could not help admiring John for his convictions.

It was about this time that John met Frank Norris, who was leading a vigorous fight against Southern Baptists and who was preaching from

time to time in Georgia. In Norris, John apparently found a champion
and after hearing Norris preach on China, said he felt called as a missionary to China."[2]

John Birch earned his B.A. at Mercer in 1939 *magna cum
laude*. From there he followed Frank Norris to Fort Worth where
Norris was establishing Bible Baptist Seminary in connection with
his church. John and another student completed the two-year
course in only one year and in July, 1940, he left for China under
the sponsorship of Norris and under the auspices of the World's
Fundamentalist Baptist Missionary Fellowship.

John managed a workable mastery of Chinese in only seven
months and began his missionary work. Following the outbreak
of war between the United States and Japan in December, 1941,
John fled the area of China heavily occupied by Japanese forces
and continued his evangelical preaching and teaching as best he
could.

Through chance circumstances, he was able to help get
Colonel Doolittle and many of his flyers out of China where they
had crash-landed following their bombing raid on Tokyo in 1942.
This service put him in touch with the 14th Air Force under
General Chennault, for whom he worked for the remainder of the
war. Using his language ability, John, now Captain John Birch,
was able to move about in China and do extensive and hazardous
intelligence work. His main task was to observe, and report by
radio, movements of Japanese troops and supplies. He carried out
his work with great courage and resourcefulness through the entire war. But on August 25, 1945, ten days after V-J Day, he met
a tragic death.

Captain Birch had volunteered to lead a party consisting of
American, Chinese Nationalist, and Korean officers and soldiers on
a special mission. The specific object of the mission has not been
disclosed, but it was into a "no man's land." The withdrawal of
the Japanese left a vacuum into which troops of both Red and
Nationalist China poured. Captain Birch and his party, traveling
by railway handcar, were stopped by a band of Red Chinese near
Hsuchow. The course of events at this point blurs. But we do know
that, in an ensuing argument with the leaders of this Red Chinese

band, Captain Birch was shot and bayoneted to death. A Chinese Nationalist officer with him was also shot and bayoneted, but lived. The others in the party were taken prisoner, but soon released. When another party left fairly soon for a mission in the same area, a member of Captain Birch's party told its new leader of the fate of the first party. He reported that Captain Birch had unwisely tried to bluff his way out of a difficult situation, that harsh words had led to insults, and insults to arrogance, and that finally the Red Chinese leader, in a fit of anger, had shot Captain Birch. Whether acting wisely or not, John Birch did die serving his country as best he knew how. He received two decorations from his country—one of them posthumously. And there, but for Robert Welch, this story of his life would have ended.

But John Birch has been lifted up by Robert Welch as his idea of the ideal Americanist; as a perfect fusion of rural virtues, fundamentalist faith, and dedicated patriotism. But why this furor? Other fine and brave soldiers lie quiet in their graves. Why single out this one? Robert Welch and the family of John Birch reply that he was deliberately murdered by the Communists and that our government deliberately kept the truth about his death from his family. The information given them was that John was killed by stray bullets. Certainly the incidents surrounding his death are obscure, but so are many deaths in war. However, the death of Captain John Birch is heavily freighted with meaning, according to Welch. It symbolizes the determination of communism to stamp out all that is fine and good in America and "exposes" the conspiracy of our national leaders in that purpose. John Birch becomes the symbol capturing, in the words of Welch, "in the story of one American boy, the ordeal of his age."[3]

All members of the John Birch Society are encouraged to read Welch's biography of their hero. There is a "Ballad of John Birch," which asks in one of its lines, "What shall we do if all our martyrs lie unresurrected and allowed to die . . . ?"[4] There is no attempt to find in his sayings or writings any further guidance or inspiration for the Society bearing his name. There are two reasons for this. First of all, the sayings and writings of a fundamentalist Baptist missionary would have rather limited appeal for an organization the membership of which, Welch reported in

1961, was 40 per cent Roman Catholic. But secondly, and more significantly, John Birch is not really the symbol of the Society at all. Robert .Welch, the founder, has become the symbol. John Birch has been reduced to a vague background figure. When the John Birch Society is mentioned, one thinks—not of John Birch, but of Robert Welch.

Who is this man?

The air crackles with excitement. The curious and near-convinced of Bakersfield, California, some seventy in number, are gathering to see whether they, too, will become disciples of Robert Welch. The banquet room of a French restaurant is the scene of frantic last-minute preparations for his coming.

Suddenly, in the midst of the final flurry, even before everyone has arrived, Robert Welch enters. He is nattily attired in a blue suit and a dark tie; he carries his dark hat, cane, and bulging brown brief case. Pale blue eyes peer through ordinary pink-rimmed glasses. He moves rather quickly through the gathering knots of people, greeting some and being introduced to others. Completing the circuit, he retires to a table near the front of the room, looks through some notes, nervously sips a glass of water. Late arrivals are ushered up to meet him. All furtively watch him as the time for the beginning of a two-day seminar draws near. A two-day "seminar" sounds fairly formidable, but unbelievably, it is actually a two-day speech.

Promptly at nine o'clock, the President of the local chamber of commerce greets us and, following further introductions and greetings, Mr. Welch rises to begin his two-day address. But it seems that the preparations are not yet complete. The speaker's stand is too low; the lights produce too much glare. Finally everything is in readiness and Robert Welch begins his own introduction. He speaks from a stack of 5 x 7 cards, which he constantly shuffles and transfers from one coat pocket to another.

He tells us that he is the bearer of bad news, that he is spending his life spreading bad news and suggests that together we "look at the score." Beginning with the inception of Russian communism, he traces its accelerating takeover of the world. A takeover not of military aggression, but of a patient gradualism, of infiltration and subversion. He is reiterating for us the *Blue Book,* his original presentation at the founding of the John Birch

Society in Indianapolis on December 8 and 9 of 1958. Occasionally he interjects additional material, but for those of us who have
read the *Blue Book,* there is little that is new. And so we sit back,
listen, and observe this mild-mannered man who has become the
center of such a storm of controversy. His delivery is flat, ponder-
ous, monotonous as he shuffles through and reads card after
card of manuscript. Perhaps for a two-day marathon—broken
only by short, disciplined coffee breaks and noonday meals—no
more exciting presentation could be expected. But there are a few
breaks in the droning monotony. We are given some diversion,
for instance, by the announcement that an uninvited reporter is
trying to get in and, frustrated in this attempt, has been reduced
to taking down the license numbers of our cars.

Despite the flatness of Welch's discourse, despite the rigid
and rigorous schedule to which we are held, we find ourselves
drawn into his spell. Gradually we come to see what drives this
man. The image which comes through in a lengthy exposure
before a friendly and attentive gathering is that of a professor
grimly and somberly emerging from his study, after having considered his observations and his conversations with those who
know, to tell his truths to those who have become dimly aware of
the foreboding, darkening skies. To these, in humility, he offers
his leadership, with a sense less of destiny than of necessity.

Robert Henry Winborne Welch, Jr., was born on a large
cotton farm in Chowan County, North Carolina, on December 1,
1899.[5] Most of his paternal ancestors were either farmers or Baptist preachers, tracing their lineage to Miles Welch, who came
to this country from Wales in 1720.

Robert Welch as a child was exposed to a strongly fundamentalist religious background. As he matured intellectually, he
rejected many of the religious concepts and doctrines which he
considered "unjustified projections of [religion's] more important
certainties."[6] He has moved religiously to a universalistic position in which he is looking for the common denominators of all
our great religions.[7] But for Welch, as for many conservatives or
liberals whose economic or political views have come to assume
the place of prime importance, religion is more to be used than
to be followed.[8]

Both his parents were college graduates and, because of the

inaccessibility of local public schools, his mother tutored her six children at home and sent them away to school only for their last two years of high school. Under this educational program, Robert Welch progressed so rapidly that he entered the University of North Carolina at the age of twelve and earned his B.A. degree at the age of seventeen. He was described as a "boy wonder" in North Carolina newspaper reports of his graduation. His other formal education includes two years at the United States Naval Academy and two years at Harvard Law School.

Welch's Business Career

While attending Law School, Robert began a candy business that so absorbed his time and energies that he left Harvard, as he had left the Naval Academy, before he graduated. In this business venture, he overextended himself and fell into financial difficulties. He invited his creditors in as an operating committee for the company, but, finding the working relationship unsatisfactory, he turned all his stock over to his creditors and pulled out. This company was eventually sold to Daggett Chocolate Company.

Welch then moved to the New York area to make another start in the candy business. Making little progress there, he was offered and accepted an executive position with E. J. Brock and Sons of Chicago. He later resigned and made one more start as a manufacturer of candy. For lack of capital, this final venture also failed. In 1934, he returned to Boston, as an employee of the James O. Welch Company, a candy manufacturing firm founded by his brother. He became one of the four vice presidents of this company and was in charge of sales and advertising, a position which took him the circuit of the sales offices of the firm in Atlanta, Pittsburgh, Chicago, Los Angeles, and Seattle.

As sales manager, Robert Welch came into close contact with business leaders in number of cities. And he moved in business circles with the prestige of seven years of membership on the Board of Directors of the National Association of Manufacturers, three years of service as a Regional Vice President, and a two-year chairmanship of its Educational Advisory Committee. His business responsibilities have also included serving as director of a bank, and as a director of several other business corporations, the Harvard Brewing Company among them. These business contacts, coupled with a lively interest in current and past political history, gave Robert Welch a very extensive circle of acquaintances across the country. Among these were not only "business" friends but also many of the anti-Socialist and anti-Communist leaders throughout the country. Consequently he could say to the first members of the Society in Indianapolis that no matter which anti-Communist or anti-Socialist group they might name, "the chances are that the good citizens who put it together are friends of mine."

In addition to extensive travel throughout this country, Mr. Welch made it a practice to use vacations and other time for world-wide junkets. Twice in England he studied "the effects of the Socialist government," and in the course of his travels he has arranged interviews with Adenauer, Chiang Kai-shek, Syngman Rhee, and others.

His Growing Involvement in Politics

Welch began to take an active part in state politics and during the 1946 campaign of Massachusetts Governor Bradford, Welch presented himself at Republican campaign headquarters, said he liked Bradford's platform and program and wanted to do his part. The man with whom he was talking leaned forward to see the size of the check Welch would write, but Welch had something else in mind. He offered to send out personal letters supporting the candidacy of Bradford to all the retail distributors and handlers of Welch candy in Massachusetts, most of whom he knew personally. Bradford's aide was pleasantly surprised. Such personal campaign material is one of the most effective ways known to gain political support for a candidate. But its cost, both in time and in the secretarial help necessary to "personalize" it, is almost prohibitive. "The costs?" Welch would take care of them himself.

The next day, Robert Welch had desks and other office equipment moved into some extra space at the campaign headquarters. He followed them in about an hour to talk with the aide about the draft of the letter he proposed to send and was, in turn, followed in about another hour by a staff of secretaries. This mailing, which approached 60,000 letters, consumed the efforts of this staff for several weeks as well as a great deal of time and effort by Welch himself. When Bradford won the campaign, Welch wanted no political favors in return.

Later, in 1950, Welch made a bid for the lieutenant governorship of Massachusetts in the Republican primary. He demonstrated a marked and rather inflexible stand for "principle," much to the dismay and chagrin of his political advisers. According to one political observer, he ran the race with tremendous drive and at a pitch very near the state of a nervous breakdown. He was then and is now a hard man to push and has an almost fanatical belief in what he's doing. In his campaign for lieutenant governor, he was always completely frank in his opinions and believed that no politician ought to compromise either as he ran for office or as he served. Such a stance flies in the face of usual political strategy and it did not win him the courted candidacy. Welch came in second in a field of four candidates, but a Democratic government was elected in Massachusetts.

Welch, however, continued to take an active part in the politics of his state, often raising or personally providing financial support for candidates. In 1952, he was strongly in favor of the presidential candidacy of Robert Taft, and tried unsuccessfully to be elected as a delegate to the Republican Convention. Although Welch didn't agree with all of Taft's views, he made twenty-five radio speeches supporting him during the primary.[10] Again, at his own expense. He shared the bitter disillusionment of many conservative Republicans when the convention by-passed Taft and nominated General Eisenhower.

Still maintaining at least a degree of faith in the conventional channels of political activity, Welch, in the same year that he founded the Birch Society, foreseeing determined liberal opposition to Goldwater's 1958 senatorial campaign in Arizona, managed to raise two thousand dollars within far-away Massachusetts to help him.[11]

But Welch was becoming increasingly discontented with the

compromise and ineffectiveness of conventional political activity. He was also becoming more and more alarmed over what he felt to be the unchecked advance of Communist subversion in this country. He himself dates his concern with the Communist conspiracy from his first reading of Eugene Lyons' *Assignment in Utopia* in 1938.[12] So we find his political interests and efforts shifting to other channels. He was a loyal supporter and has been a faithful memorializer of the late Senator Joseph McCarthy. He addressed state gatherings of "friends of Senator Joseph McCarthy" at least twice in 1955, and in 1956 made an address at a States Righters Conference which met in Memphis and nominated T. Coleman Andrews for President and Thomas H. Werdel for Vice President.

In addition to his other activities, Robert Welch is a prolific writer. Between 1959 and 1963, for instance, Welch himself estimates that his output totaled more than a half million words.[14] His first book, *The Road to Salesmanship,* a fairly standard "how-to-do-it-yourself" handbook, was published in 1941. As he began to move into right-wing politics, Henry Regnery Company in 1952 published *May God Forgive Us,* Welch's analysis of the dismissal of General MacArthur by President Truman. (Interestingly enough this book was published as a "letter," a literary form later used by Welch in the "private letter," more than twice as long, entitled *The Politician.*) During 1952, reportedly 185,000 paper-bound and 9,000 hard-bound copies of the book on MacArthur were printed. In 1954, *The Life of John Birch* was published, and, according to Welch, ran to 35,000 paper-bound and 3,000 hard-bound copies. Both *May God Forgive Us* and *The Life of John Birch* have since been reprinted as issues of *American Opinion.* In February, 1956, Welch embarked upon a new venture. He began to edit and publish a magazine entitled *One Man's Opinion,* which was issued somewhat irregularly and which had only a few thousand readers. The title of this publication was changed to *American Opinion* upon the founding of the John Birch Society two years later.

American Opinion has been somewhat of a problem child because, for at least its first four years, including the two years under the title of *One Man's Opinion,* it was in the red financially.

Welch turned all his stock in the magazine over to the Birch
Society when he began "seeing signs" that the magazine would
soon start making money, so that when, or if, this happened there
would be no grounds for a charge that he was getting rich from
this aspect of the Birch Society operation. The charge made at
the time Welch did turn over this stock, that he was just unload-
ing a financial liability upon the Birch Society, is apparently
groundless. According to Welch, the gift of the stock involved the
Society in no financial responsibility for the support of the magazine, but only insured that potential profit from it would go to
the Society instead of to himself.[15] But whether *American Opinion*
is profit-making or not, it is interesting to note that financial reports
and audits are not issued to the members of the Society. Since June,
1960, there has been a fairly sustained drive to get members of the
Society either to subscribe to *American Opinion* (formerly $5.00,
now $10.00, per year) or to write asking for a free "charity" sub-
scription. More recently, there has been an attempt to upgrade
quality, interest, and income for this magazine with employment
of a full-time managing editor and a business manager.

With its February, 1964, issue, *American Opinion* featured
on its cover, not a picture of one of the prominent persons
considered by Welch to be a "conscious or unconscious agent
of the Communist conspirary," but the first of a projected
series of portraits of "great Americans." This projected cover
series may simply be a stopgap until the next national election—until there are some new faces to place on the cover
and some new names to smear inside—but I think not. This emphasis on "great Americans" would seem rather to be one more
evidence of the attempt by the Birch Society to project a "more
positive" and more "respectable" image.

The great American featured on this first cover is "naturally," according to the introductory notes of Robert Welch, "General Douglas MacArthur." The general's former aide, Colonel
Laurence E. Bunker, allegedly the second-in-line for the leadership of the Birch Society, makes the following tribute to
MacArthur:

Brilliant military strategist, wise and compassionate administrator
of a conquered people, cogent exponent of the principles that built this

nation into the mightiest in history, elder statesman unsurpassed in his understanding of his country's great potential and the forces that would cramp and curtail its progress toward even greater leadership in mankind's drive for liberty under law, General of the Army Douglas MacArthur exemplifies the basic ideals and objectives which *American Opinion* seeks to expound and promote.

The approach of the February issue is quite typical. Robert Welch's opening remarks conclude with a tribute to *American Opinion.* "In an age when the objects of reverence are gradually diminishing, it is our firm purpose to be selective in the material which appears inside the attractive covers. For we plan to make *American Opinion* the most authoritative magazine, here or abroad, on the real significance of contemporary events, trends, and personalities which are determining our future.

"With this purpose in mind, we continue to welcome your praise, your interest, and your criticisms. And new subscriptions for those still unaware of—but searching for—American Opinion."

The lead article is by the former Congressman from California, now Western District Governor of the Society, John Rousselot. He discusses civil rights as a "Communist betrayal of a good cause." Rousselot contends "that fomentation of conflict between the races in America has been a key program of the Communist Party U.S.A. for many years." He makes a number of unsubstantiated assertions cast in the "form" of a factual argument. He raises the twin specters of "states rights" and "property rights" and gives counsels of patience and prudence to the American Negro.

Next follow current quotes from well-known personages entitled "They Paused to Remark." There are quotes from both the "good guys" and the "bad guys" including: Norman Thomas, Nikita Khrushchev, Lyndon B. Johnson (who "tipped his hand" by saying, "And more than ever we must support the United Nations, as the best instrument yet devised to promote the peace of the world and the well-being of mankind."), J. Edgar Hoover, Adlai Stevenson, Dean Rusk, Chou En-lai, Linus Pauling, and General Douglas MacArthur.

"Marxmanship in Dallas" is the topic of Revilo P. Oliver, a Professor of Classics in the University of Illinois, and a regular contributor to *American Opinion*. He maintains that "there are two basic reasons why the American people were shocked and grieved by the assassination. Neither has anything to do with either the personal character of the victim or the identity of the assassin." Mr. Oliver considers these two reasons to be: (1) "The victim was the President of the United States; he was therefore symbolically representative of the nation, and his assassination was a form of armed attack on our country." (2) "Regardless of office, political violence is always shocking and a warning of impending collapse."

One possible explanation offered by Mr. Oliver for the assassination of President Kennedy by the Communists (the Birch Society has taken the line that Oswald was a Communist "acting under orders") was that he was "planning to turn American." Mr. Oliver goes on to say that "if Kennedy did entertain laudable designs, he cannot have kept them entirely *in petto* [Italian for "secret"]; he must have disclosed them to a few persons, perhaps including his father, in whom he had confidence. And if he did, the time for these persons to give evidence is now, while there is still a chance to clear the reputation of the deceased." Such tasteless trash neither needs nor merits editorial comment.

Charles Callan Tansill next gives an informative study of "The Real Story of the Berlin Blockade."

The reader is given a short "lesson" in "Principles of Economics" by Hans Sennholz, according to whom, "profit sharing," presented as "the key to industrial peace," has the possibility of a great many drawbacks for the workingman, not to mention his employer—which he doesn't.

"If You Want It Straight," you shouldn't turn to Robert Welch's column in this issue, for you will find a rambling, disjointed, and banal commentary on the criminality of rulers (especially Communists in general, and Jomo Kenyatta in particular), on the government's study on smoking, and a closing paragraph on Herbert Spencer.

The next section protects the reader against misconceptions he may have gained through the "Communistically controlled" mass media. As a corrective, the magazine is out to "get" Governor Nelson Rockefeller. But considering the fact that he is competing for the Republican presidential nomination against their man, and that he has added unforgivable insult to injury by challenging Goldwater to rational debate, the ire of *American Opinion* is understandable.

Even the Arts have found a place in the pages of *American Opinion*. Jack Moffitt has some rather good book and movie reviews, only slightly interlarded with commentary on the international Communist conspiracy.

Martin Dies, the man who was given credit in the Society's post-assassination ads as the one who declared that Oswald was "a Communist," gives the history of "The War On Anti-Communists." It seems that anti-Communists have always been persecuted, especially by the "Liberal Front," which Dies promises to describe in a later article. This should be good news for those who aren't being persecuted, but who feel deep down inside as though they ought to be. They can join the Birch Society!

Next are "Bullets," comments both serious and tongue-in-cheek. Theodore Roosevelt is quoted as saying: "The first requisite of a good citizen in this republic of ours is that he should be willing and able to pull his own weight." And from the *Gibbon Gazette* we learn that: "The huge national debt our younger generation will inherit should keep them from one indulgence —ancestor worship."

Westbrook Pegler in his first column after the assassination of President Kennedy makes no mention of the event. He has written a fairly harmless and fairly amusing column on Damon Runyon. Perhaps the best thing that could be said about Mr. Oliver's article on the assassination would be that Pegler was not allowed to write it.

Taylor Caldwell, "the most widely read author in the world" the reader is told, writes a heart-rending article stating that "The Heart Of Man Is Cold." It seems that anyone who's not a Communist or a "liberal"—especially anyone who's a loyal American— finds himself out in the cold. She wants her readers to keep up the fight, but she's going to try to go back to the God of her Sunday-school childhood to try to learn to trust again. . . .

By this time the reader is beginning to run into the ads.

There is a page of jokes entitled "Confetti," with all the sophisti-
cation of those in *Boy's Life*. Running through the ads is "A
Review of the News" day by day for the past month. These short
items serve largely to keep the reader informed of the daily
progress of the Communist conspiracy. One of the items for December 7 looks particularly sinister: "According to the *New York
Times*, former President Eisenhower has asked Ambassador Henry
Cabot Lodge to be a candidate for the Republican Presidential
nomination in 1964."

There are two ads supporting the so-called Liberty Amendment: one giving its story "to every person interested in his own
well-being, and in the future of his children;" another by Spin-
dale Cotton Mills, which also "exposes" income tax as a plot of
Karl Marx.

There is a regular full-page ad of Allen-Bradley, advertising
electrical switches which appear to be in no way related to the
international Communist conspiracy.

The Circuit Riders urge you to write in and get the book
that may expose your clergyman. He may be a Com-symp!

"The American Opinion Speakers Bureau" has a two-page
spread giving pictures and write-ups on ten speakers. In this lay-
out they are well covered against any charges of discrimination:
there is a Negro, a Jew, a woman, a Rhodes Scholar, and one
young man who is under fifty.

If "your friends need *proof*," "We The People" will send
you or them (for 50¢) a startling 32-page transcript: "The Best
Kept Secrets of the New Frontier." Satisfaction is guaranteed.

The Politician rates a full-page ad and its price is down
from eight to two dollars.

Some tract-printing house has gotten in on anticommunism
and they offer thirty post cards with different messages (or fifty
with one) for $1.00. "Also *Thugs and Communists*, the book
proving Communism the most dangerous criminal conspiracy the
world has ever known." Hard-bound $5.10, paperback, only $2.00.

There is one ad announcing a limited edition of a tribute
in verse, "The Ballad of John Birch" to be published March 15.
No price is indicated. (Four stanzas of the Ballad are on the last
page facing Colonel Bunker's tribute to General MacArthur.)

Next there is one page of letters to the editor, and one page of poetry edited by E. Merrill Root.

An ad on the back cover pictures a bloody sword held by a taloned hand being thrust through the Dominican Republic. General Arturo Espaillat has written a book entitled *Trujillo: The Last Caesar* which sells for $4.95.

The *Bulletin* is a monthly booklet that goes to each member of the John Birch Society. It is edited and almost wholly written by Welch. In it are shorter statements analyzing and documenting (to Welch's satisfaction) the nature and progress of the Communist conspiracy. There are also reports of progress on continuing and past items that have been on the agenda for action by the Society. But the central part of each *Bulletin* is the "Agenda for the Month," its items consisting largely of letters to be written either in protest against or in support of some action or person. They exhort the members to further study of the nature of the Communist conspiracy as it can be seen in lists of "approved" books and urge them to hand this educational material on to their friends and acquaintances. In addition, there are listed a wide variety of short-term or long-term national and local campaigns and activities, such as the campaign to "Impeach Earl Warren."

As one can see, Robert Welch, moving further and further toward the right, has become an ambitious author and a prolific pamphleteer. Implicit in all his writing is a theory of organization and leadership which we need to examine to understand the society which he founded.

The American Dilemma as Perceived by Welch

Welch's theory of leadership gains its authoritarian character and its driving sense of urgency from his understanding of the dilemma faced by our country. He paints a very grim picture of the international conquests of communism that have been recognized by our government as well as what he considers *de facto* ones as yet unacknowledged.[16] He also paints a grim picture of Communistic infiltration into our government. For example, during the Eisenhower administration, Welch wrote that in his judgment, the Communists had "one of their own" as President. And what have we with which to oppose this advance of communism? According to Welch's understanding "At present we are in the position of trying to defeat a disciplined well-armed expertly-commanded army with a collection of debating societies. And it can't be done."[17] (The dubious assumption of this statement is that the American right wing is the counterpart of the threat of international communism, not the FBI and our armed forces.)

Welch sees the country as nearly overwhelmed. What solution does he then propose? He insists that only a truly dedicated and unified minority, the John Birch Society under his personal leadership, is capable of stopping and reversing the Communist tide. He hopes that the Birch Society will be "the moving force for a new age."[18] And he believes that it can be. For he holds that the course of "history is always determined by minorities who really know what they want."[19]

The Charismatic Leader

But how can a minority exercise effective influence? In the *Blue Book* chapter entitled "Under Positive Leadership," Welch builds his own image of "dynamic personal leadership."[20] According to him, the lack of dominant and unifying leadership explains the splintering tendencies and the general ineffectiveness of the American right wing. A minority which aspires to alter the course of history must center membership loyalty upon the leader, not upon the organization. Welch draws out this concept of leadership particularly in his discussion of the differences between a group functioning as an "organization" and as a "body."

Welch conceives an "organization" to be "a collection of individuals or groups held together more or less loosely and more or less temporarily by a common interest or common objective."[21] A "body," as he sees it, "is an organic entity." There seem to be two main points in this distinction: the first is that the members of a group organized as a "body" can move quickly and in concert; the second is that, to gain these advantages of rapid and forceful

action upon a wide variety of issues and over an extended period
of time, members must forego the "attractions" of a republican
form of organization[22] and willingly take their assigned places
along a chain of command. The "head" of the "body," the top
link in the chain of command is, of course, the leader. Comparing
our country with a shoreline of beautiful houses about to be
flooded, Welch feels that the leader who hopes to unify the now
scattered and sporadic efforts of the American right wing, must be
a "hardboiled, dictatorial, and dynamic boss." He feels that, if
under such leadership, "everybody puts everything he's got into
the job without stopping to argue, we'll be able to save [our
country] from this incoming flood."

The "Search" for the Leader

Who, then, is this leader to be? As Welch considered this
with the men who met in Indianapolis to hear about forming the
Birch Society, he reviewed some likely candidates for the position.
Barry Goldwater was a highly esteemed possibility. Welch said of
his qualifications:

> Barry Goldwater has political know-how and the painstaking genius
> to use that know-how with regard to infinite details. He is a superb polit-
> ical organizer, and inspires deep and lasting loyalty. He is absolutely
> sound in his Americanism, has the political and moral courage to stand by
> his Americanist principles, and in my opinion can be trusted to stand by
> them till hell freezes over.[23]

But despite all these sterling qualities, Welch felt that
Goldwater was too tightly bound within his political framework
of action to offer the overall [sic] leadership needed. Even if Goldwater was successful in the political arena, to the extent of being
elected President, Welch believed that he would still not be able
to carry the fight against the Communists through the political
sphere alone; he would still need the support of leadership on
other fronts. Welch mentioned, in passing, that the same would
be the case for Bill Knowland or Bill Jenner or any one of a

dozen others upon the political front. Having discarded Goldwater, Welch moved on to a scathing "consideration" of Richard
Nixon:

As for being a leader, the sad truth, hard for many hopeful and
wishful conservative Republicans to realize, is that Richard Nixon, a most
engaging personality and clever politician, has never been a *leader* in
connection with any event or development, or at any stage of his career.
He has been a rider of waves, so far as public support was concerned, without caring whether the particular wave at any given time was moving left
or right; and a manipulator, of uncanny skill, behind the scenes.[24]

Welch said further that if it were not for

. . . the dirtiest deal in American political history, participated in if not actually engineered by Richard Nixon in order to make himself Vice-Presi-
dent (and to put Warren on the Supreme Court as part of that deal),
Taft would have been nominated at Chicago in 1952. It is almost certain
that Taft would have been elected President by a far greater plurality
than was Eisenhower, that a grand rout of the Communists in our government and in our midst would have started, that McCarthy would be alive
today, and that we wouldn't even be in this mess that we're supposed to
look to Nixon to lead us out of.[25]

This is a rather remarkable catalogue of right-wing grievances. A great deal of right-wing disillusionment with "politics"
dates back to the selection by the 1952 Republican Convention
of the popular but politically naïve Eisenhower over their nearly
"purist" conservative champion, Taft. This material on Nixon
has been deleted from later editions of the *Blue Book* since
February, 1961. A second major grievance centers in the "Warren"
Supreme Court School Desegregation decision of 1954. This decision itself is seldom mentioned but the "underlying" arguments
against it are standard tenets of right-wing dogma.

Welch further indicted Nixon for the defeat of Knowland
in the latter's bid for the governorship of California in 1958. But
he went on to say that Nixon, nevertheless, might remain the
best possibility for the presidential nomination in 1960.

Welch concluded this discussion of other possible leaders for the John Birch Society by pressing the idea that politicians cannot be counted upon for this task.

> We shall have to use politicians, support politicians, create politicians, and help the best ones we can find to get elected. I am thoroughly convinced, however, that we cannot count on politicians, political leadership, or even political action except as a part of something much deeper and broader, to save us.[26]

Having largely disqualified politicians as a group from possible leadership of the John Birch Society, it is very interesting that Welch did not go on to consider the possibilities of existing non-political leadership within the American right wing. J. B. Matthews, an adviser to Welch, was not considered. The late Alfred Kohlberg, Clarence Manion, Colonel Laurence E. Bunker, and the less well-known S. M. Draskovich—all men selected by Welch for membership on the Council of the John Birch Society—were not even mentioned. In 1958, at the time of the formation of the Society, recently defeated William Knowland, or General MacArthur would have been possibilities. Neither was there any apparent consideration, for this task of over-all leadership, of newly established men such as William F. Buckley, Fulton Lewis, Jr., Dan Smoot, Fred Schwarz, Billy James Hargis, or of such established right-wingers as Gerald L. K. Smith, Carl McIntire, Edward C. Bundy, John T. Flynn or E. Merrill Root.

With the career of Senator McCarthy undoubtedly in the back of his mind, Welch for a time considered running for the U.S. Senate. But further thought and study led him to the conclusion that

> (1) No one outspoken Senator nor a dozen outspoken Senators, and no amount of the ephemeral political support they might muster, could possibly save our country unless there was, encompassing them and their efforts and support, this far larger and broader movement to which I keep referring; (2) That there was not going to be any movement without the dynamic overall [sic] personal leadership to which I have been referring; and (3) that, with all of my own shortcomings, there wasn't anybody else on the horizon willing to give their whole lives to the job, with the determination and dedication I would put into it. . . .[27]

Welch buttressed his qualifications for leadership in two ways. First of all, he "knew those who know"; he was acquainted with both national and international anti-Communist leaders.

Not only did he claim to know "those who know" but, secondly, he claimed another qualification for leadership because of a "knowledge" and "understanding" of the Communistic conspiracy that was deeper and broader than that of most conservative or anti-Communist leaders. This claim was made early in the *Blue Book* and was reiterated many times. A case in point would be his criticism of Goldwater for going along with the Republican ticket of Nixon and Lodge which ran on the platform demanded by Rockefeller. In failing to repudiate this ticket and in failing to lead a conservative coalition of both parties into a third "American Party," Welch felt that Goldwater missed "a rendezvous with history which it was a tragedy for him not to keep." Welch also stated that "the Communists are much further advanced and more deeply entrenched than is realized by even most of the serious students of the danger among the anti-Communists."[28] Welch noted, too, that:

I personally have been studying the problem increasingly for about nine years, and practically full time for the past three years. And entirely without pride, but in simple thankfulness, let me point out that a lifetime of business experience should have made it easier for me to see the falsity of the economic theories on which Communism is supposedly based, more readily, than might some scholar coming into that study from the academic cloisters; while a lifetime of interest in things academic, especially world history, should have given me an advantage over many businessmen, in more readily seeing the sophistries in dialectic materialism. So I have felt, rightly or wrongly, that my grasp of Communist purposes, and even of their methods, should have been more rapid than some of my patriotic friends who have gradually become staunch anti-Communists.[29]

This claim to have deeper and broader knowledge and insight than other leaders was perhaps most dramatically put forth in publications such as the July, August, and September, 1960, issues of *American Opinion* entitled, "A World Gone Crazy: A panoramic survey of the degree of Communist influence in each of 107 countries," and in the February, 1962, issue entitled "Calling the Shots," which is a record of "past insight" at times when, in the words of Welch, "The whole regiment seemed out of step but us!"

According to Welch, he was the leader that the anti-Communists needed. And he believed that only a large, tightly organized group, under the direction of a "personal" leader in whose leadership the members had absolute confidence and to whom they gave "unshakable" loyalty could possibly counter the Communist advance that he perceived nationally and internationally. Such an organization, a "body" must be created to counter this threat and Welch proceeded to create it.

CHAPTER III

Appointed Senators of a Private Forum

A reporter entered the red brick building at 395 Concord Avenue, Belmont, walked down the narrow corridor and poked his head into the large brightly lighted office.

A young lady arose from her desk and said, "Can I help you?"

"Yes, could I see Mr. Welch, please?"

The lady asked his name and then said, "I'm sorry, but Mr. Welch is very busy."

"How long do you suppose he'll be tied up?" asked the reporter.

"At least a month," she said.

Staggered, the reporter reflected a second, and then remarked, "Lady, no one can be that busy."

"Well, he is," she said. "And we are."[1]

Robert Welch and the organization he designed and built have, indeed, been busy. What sort of an organization is it? Welch in late 1958, when he founded the Society, described it as follows:

> The John Birch Society will function almost entirely through small local chapters, usually of from ten to twenty dedicated patriots, although some chapters may occasionally, and for a while, be larger. Each will have a Chapter Leader, appointed by headquarters, which is in Belmont, Massachusetts; or appointed through officers of the Society, in the field, who have themselves been duly appointed by headquarters. The dues are whatever the member wants to make them, with a minimum of $24.00 per year for men and $12.00 per year for women. But we shall prefer to have these dues paid by each member of a local chapter monthly, at $2.00 per month for men and $1.00 per month for women, to his or her Chapter Leader. This is for many reasons, some of which are obvious and it will be the responsibility of each Chapter Leader to collect such dues regularly and forward them to headquarters.[2]

44

The chapters of the Society grow in number in two ways. First, by being organized upon the initiative of either a prospective chapter leader or organizer ("co-ordinator"). Second, by division into two chapters when the first reaches about twenty members. In addition to the regular monthly dues, "life memberships" are offered at one thousand dollars. The collection of the regular dues and the prescribed monthly meetings, where the monthly *Bulletin* is read and explained, both serve as fairly reliable checks for the home office on the "live" interest of members.

Welch proposed "Home Chapter" memberships to provide for people who would want to join the Society, but who lived in localities where there were not yet local chapters.

Regular local chapter leaders were expected to meet with the members in their chapters at least once a month and on any special occasions which seemed advisable in order to carry out directives issued from the home office headquarters. Chapter leaders were also expected to keep in almost continuous contact with members between chapter meetings to further these concerted efforts.

To supervise chapter leaders and to form new chapters, paid organizers called co-ordinators were to be used. Above the co-ordinators, there were eventually to be major co-ordinators. Thus there would be a direct chain of command from headquarters through the major co-ordinators, co-ordinators, and chapter leaders to the members. This would provide ". . . strict and careful control of what every chapter is doing, and every member of every chapter so far as the effective work of the John Birch Society is concerned."[3]

According to "A Frank Report" which was mailed out to the members of the society with their *Bulletin* for July, 1963, there were forty members in this field staff of "co-ordinators."

While recognizing the necessity of paying salary and expenses for the co-ordinators, Welch stated that "neither the top leadership, including himself, nor the bottom leadership level of chapter leaders would receive any pay at all."[4] Welch seems to have failed to anticipate the large clerical and administrative staff which has developed at the home office.

Among the group of "top officers," who, along with Welch,

received no pay, are included members of the "Council" of the Society. The core of this group was ten of the eleven men who met with Robert Welch at the founding of the Society in Indianapolis in December of 1958.

In addition to the forty co-ordinators, according to "A Frank Report" the other paid staff includes sixty-four members of the office staff at the home office in Belmont; nine at the office overseen by former Congressman John Rousselot in San Marino, California; seven on the staff of the American Opinion Speakers Bureau in Brookfield, Massachusetts; and four other secretaries for the "major co-ordinators" in other parts of the country.

We are out to get a million members truly dedicated to the things in which we believe. This, we are well aware, will take time, and tremendous effort, and dedication on our own part greater than that we ask of anybody else. But there are a million good patriots, who are also men and women of good will and good character and human conscience in America, who are just waiting to join The John Birch Society as fast as we can carry the story to them. There are a million such men and women in America who would join The John Birch Society tonight if they knew as much about it as you men in this room do right now. And I think that a million members is all we would want, at least in the United States. For we need disciplined pullers at the oars, and not passengers in the boat.[5]

After three years of organizational effort, this goal of a million members was modified to a goal of 100,000 to be reached by the end of 1961 (according to The Los Angeles *Times*, March 5, 1961). Since the Society refuses to reveal its membership, estimates of its current total membership are largely guesswork. During the "tour" of the home office, which I described in the Introduction, I made a rough estimate of the number of *Bulletins* piled up and ready for mailing. These *Bulletins* are mailed to each member. My rough estimate of bundles including 20 to 30 *Bulletins* each, stacked in 30 rows, 4 bundles high and 5 bundles across, would place the membership at from 12,000 to 18,000. This figure corresponds closely to one drawn from a financial report of the Society for 1962 filed with the Attorney General of Massachusetts, which gave the total income from dues as $296,326. I would estimate that women ($12 dues per year) outnumber men ($24 dues

per year) by two to one. This calculation places the total membership in 1962 at 16,463. But, if the current drive to double the
number of field co-ordinators is successful, the membership is
bound to increase.

On paper, this is the organizational structure of the Birch
Society. Among the currently proliferating right-wing groups, it
is by far the best organized.

The organization is designed by Welch to utilize what he
feels to be the strengths of "dynamic *personal* leadership around
which the split and frustrated and confused forces on our side can
be rallied, rapidly and firmly. . . ." In line with this conviction
as to the utility and necessity of "charismatic" leadership, Welch
insists that the Birch Society is to be a "monolithic body." He
goes on to make what has been, next to his statement in *The
Politician* that Eisenhower is a "conscious agent of the Communist
conspiracy" probably the most disturbing statement of organizational and political philosophy that he has ever made:

> A republican form of government or of organization has many at-
> tractions and advantages, *under certain* [unstated] *favorable conditions.
> But under less happy circumstances* it lends itself too readily to infiltra-
> tion, distortion and disruption. And democracy, of course, in government
> or organization, as the Greeks and Romans both found out, and as I be-
> lieve every man in this room clearly recognizes—democracy is merely a
> deceptive phrase, a weapon of demagoguery, and a perennial fraud.[6]

Welch goes on for the next three pages of the *Blue Book*
to say that this antidemocratic, authoritarian stance applies, not
to government, but to the organization of the Birch Society alone
and is intended primarily to guard against infiltration by Communists and against divisive debate leading to internal splintering
of the Society. But the weight of his original statement explicitly
includes and elaborates upon his political philosophy of government.

The Leader

For the Birch Society under these "less happy circumstances,"
Robert Welch has designated himself very clearly as the unchal-

lengeable leader. But his leadership has, in fact, been considerably modified by others in the chain of command.

The Council

The Council of the John Birch Society was the only group of advisers with which Welch had originallly planned to contend. They were enlisted partly from the eleven men who met with Welch at the founding of the Society. Welch, himself described their function as threefold:

(1) To show the stature and the standing of the leadership of the Society; (2) to give your Founder the benefit of the Council's advice and guidance, both in procedural and organizational matters, and in substantive matters of policy; and (3) to select, with absolute and final authority, a Successor to myself as head of the John Birch Society, if and when an accident, "suicide," or anything sufficiently fatal is arranged for me by the Communists—or I simply die in bed of old age and a cantankerous disposition.[7]

The ninth and latest edition of the *Blue Book* gives a list of the membership of the Council which is somewhat out of date. After consultation with the Belmont office in February, 1964, I have omitted four who have left the Council and three who are deceased, and have added four new members. The information on each man is from Birch Society sources.

Dr. N. E. Adamson, Jr. A Boston surgeon. Assistant Medical Director of New England Mutual Life Insurance Company. Youngest member of the Council in 1961.

Mr. Thomas J. Anderson. Editor and Publisher of *Farm and Ranch,* farm paper with 1,300,000 circulation.

Hon. T. Coleman Andrews. Former Commissioner of Internal Revenue of the United States. Now Chairman of the Board of two large (and affiliated) insurance companies.

Mr. Frank Cullen Brophy, Phoenix, Arizona, has been a president of five banks; a philanthropist, civic leader, and cattleman; President of a nationally known food-packing company, President of a huge grocery combine, and vice president of an Arizona mining company; considers himself a Jeffersonian Democrat, author of a book on politics entitled *Though Far Away*; is highly regarded in investment banking circles,

Col. Laurence E. Bunker. Former Personal Aide to General Douglas MacArthur for 6½ years—during the Japanese occupation, the Korean War, and MacArthur's early months in this country after his return.

Mr. F. Gano Chance. President, A. B. Chance Company, Centralia, Missouri. Former President of Missouri Chamber of Commerce and of Associated Industries of Missouri.

Mr. S. J. Conner. President of the Conroth Company, Chicago, and with many other business interests.

Mr. Ralph E. Davis. President of General Plant Protection Corporation and affiliated companies, Los Angeles.

Dr. S. M. Draskovich. Author of *Tito, Moscow's Trojan Horse*. Editor-in-chief of *Srpska Borba* (*The Serbian Struggle*), a weekly newspaper, published in Chicago, with sizable circulation in thirty-six countries.

Father Francis E. Fenton, a Roman Catholic priest of Bridgeport, Connecticut.

Mr. Wm. J. Grede. President of Grede Foundries, Inc., Milwaukee. Former President of the National Association of Manufacturers and former head of the International YMCA.

Mr. A. G. Heinsohn, Jr. President, Cherokee Mills, Sevierville, Tennessee. Author of *One Man's Fight For Freedom*. A very successful manufacturer and a very dedicated patriot.

Mr. Fred C. Koch. President, Rock Island Oil and Refining Company, Wichita, Kansas. Strong supporter of many patriotic movements, and especially of right-to-work legislation.

Mr. Robert D. Love, Wichita, Kansas, Vice President of the Love Box Company, who has been active in state and local associations and Chambers of Commerce, and who served five years on the Board of Directors of the National Association of Manufacturers. He was one of the founders of the Kansas Right to Work organization and has long been an active leader in the National Right to Work Committee. He has also been active for many years in YMCA work, and has served for the past several years as Chairman of the Board of Trustees of the Wichita Metropolitan YMCA.

Dean Clarence Manion. Former Dean of Notre Dame Law School.

In 1954 resigned from important government appointment rather than stop crusading for the Bricker Amendment. Founded the Manion Forum, which now reaches a huge nationwide radio audience every week.

Mr. N. Floyd McGowin. President, W. T. Smith Lumber Company, Chapman, Alabama. Active on many important boards of national organizations and enterprises.

Mr. W. B. McMillan. President of the Hussmann Refrigerator Company, St. Louis, Missouri. An outstanding business leader. Was, next to your Founder, the first member of the John Birch Society.

Robert H. Montgomery, a prominent Boston lawyer and author of *The Murder and the Myth,* a study of the famous Sacco-Vanzetti case.

Dr. Revilo P. Oliver. Professor of Classical Languages and Literatures at the University of Illinois. Recognized as one of the very top scholars in America in his field. One of the ablest speakers on the Americanist side.

Hon. M. T. Phelps. Former Chief Justice of the Supreme Court of Arizona.

Mr. Louis Ruthenburg. Formerly President, then Chairman of the Board, of Servel, Inc., Evansville, Indiana. Former President, Indiana State Chamber of Commerce. Now retired except as an industrial consultant. Has received several honorary degrees and three Freedom Foundation awards.

Mr. J. Nelson Shepherd. President, Midwest-Beach Co., Sioux Falls, South Dakota. An outstanding citizen and strong supporter of many patriotic causes.

Mr. Robert W. Stoddard. President of Wyman-Gordon Company, Worcester, Massachusetts. On board of directors of several of New England's largest businesses, including First National Bank of Boston. Has just served two terms as President of Associated Industries of Massachusetts. Active on the boards of many educational and philanthropic institutions.

Lt. General Charles B. Stone, III, U. S. A. F. (Retired) . Succeeded General Claire Chennault as Commander of our 14th Airforce, in China, and is lifetime Honorary Chairman of the 14th Airforce Association.

I have talked at length with a fourth of the members of the Council, an interesting and varied group.[8] If Robert Welch finds himself getting more "advice" from his Council than he bargained for, it should be no surprise to him, for none of these men appear to have any shortage of opinions.

Colonel Laurence Bunker, the Council member who has been described as the next in line for leadership of the Society, resides on a quiet, winding, tree-lined street in the Boston suburb of Wellesley. His home is a spacious, but properly unpretentious house that belonged to his father. Colonel Bunker is a distin-guished-looking and very well-spoken man about the same age as Welch. During the Second World War, he served as an aide to General MacArthur and shared the General's glory, his frustrat-ing leadership of the Korean War, his humiliation and anger over his recall by President Truman, and his bitterness when both he and Taft were passed over by the 1952 Republican Con-vention in favor of General Eisenhower. Understandably perhaps, Bunker was on hand at the Indianapolis meeting in 1958 when the Birch Society, a movement of protest, was founded. He was, interestingly enough, one of the two men who didn't sign up immediately, but he did join later. Such caution is perhaps char-acteristic of this man for, despite the fact that he is spoken of as heir apparent to the leadership of Welch, Bunker's caution and calmness are outwardly much in contrast to Welch's impetuosity. Probably Bunker often gives Welch counsels of moderation. For in-stance, Bunker has long opposed the Society's "Movement to Impeach Earl Warren." He believes that the basic "trouble with the Supreme Court" is not subversion, but the appointment of inexperienced and unqualified men to its bench. Bunker is, there-fore, in favor of legislative enactment of a set of criteria, including extensive previous legal experience, for candidates being con-sidered for appointment to the Court. He believes that a drive to establish such criteria should replace or at least be promoted parallel to the "movement" to impeach Warren.

But, in contrast to advising caution regarding the Supreme Court, Bunker urged Welch to publish the controversial letter, *The Politician,* to show how little difference there has been in the Presidential Administrations of Roosevelt, Truman, Eisenhower, and Kennedy.

Fred C. Koch of Wichita, a man in his early sixties and one of the wealthiest men in Kansas, is another man well near the top of the Birch Society hierarchy. Besides membership in the Council, he is also on its Executive Committee. Mr. Koch became acquainted with the Russian Communists early in his career when his firm helped set up several oil-cracking plants in Russia during the first Soviet five-year plan. He saw the creation of a police state in Soviet Russia with "every fourth person" in the hierarchy of power serving as a spy upon his fellows. He was further alarmed when he heard from an old hard-core Bolshevik, a man who was later shot during the Stalinist "purges," of the Communist plans to infiltrate the schools, universities, churches, labor unions, government, and armed forces of the U.S.A.[9] Fred Koch at last found in the Birch Society an organization which he felt might be capable of destroying the advances that he believes the Communists have made in their plans for subversion of this country. He has supplied most of the funds for the Birch Society effort in Wichita, including funds for an abortive attempt to set up a "patriotic" bookstore. The basement trophy room of his palatial estate serves as a meeting place for the Society in Wichita and Koch is deeply involved and committed in his local leadership of the Birch Society, but he is pessimistic. As I talked with him he expressed the fear that "we are losing the battle," that "the way things are going, we'll be down the drain by 1967 or 1970."

As he brought this somber view to focus on the effectiveness of the Birch Society, Koch was very critical of Welch's leadership. He didn't feel that Welch should be replaced, but he criticized him for trying to assume too much leadership himself. The job is too big for one man, no matter how well qualified, Koch thought, and he felt that Welch must delegate a great deal more responsibility to others.

Frank Cullen Brophy lives in an attractive whitewashed adobe, red-tile-roofed, Spanish-style home on the outskirts of Phoenix. His office and waiting room over the garage are comfortably furnished and finished in natural wood. As Mr. Brophy gave final instructions to an assistant, I peered around the waiting room which was bedecked with pictures and relics of the Western frontier. One plaque caught my eye: "Of all human ambitions an open mind eagerly expectant of new discoveries and ready to remould convictions in the light of the added knowledge and dispelled ignorances and misconceptions, is the noblest, the rarest and the most difficult to achieve."

Brophy, an energetic man in his late sixties with a vivid complexion set off by white hair and mustache, immediately set me straight on his political affiliation. He said he was a Jeffersonian Democrat. It seems that Jefferson, in his conflict with Madison, tried to establish an agrarian democracy, but since this had degenerated into an industrial mobocracy, Brophy left the Democratic party in 1952.

There is a theory held by many political scientists that those on our political right wing are fighting against the anti-individualistic depersonalization of "bigness" in all its forms. Frank Brophy was the only man I interviewed who was clear-cut in his distaste for bigness. He was not only against big labor and big government, but his individualistic frontier nature rebelled even against big business.

He stated that only Texas and Arizona have any pioneer spirit left. Free enterprise has been given free rein and until recently there have been no big corporations in Arizona except mines; the majority of the people have been small individual proprietors. Therefore, he concluded, these states will probably be the last ones to go under.

Brophy thought that the conservative movement, of which the Birch Society is a part, is basically a protest by people over the loss of individuality. Discussing liberals and conservatives, he said that most liberals don't know what the hell they're doing; they don't think straight; they want *everybody* to be happy and prosperous; fuzzy thinking. But conservatives are practical, hardheaded, realistic; they can think a lot straighter than a liberal. He does grant, however, that both liberals and conservatives have good motives and want to do right.

Somehow the alleged wealth of the right wing came up, perhaps with mention of H. L. Hunt. Anyway, Brophy maintained that the extremely rich (along with the extremely poor) are on the *other* side, that the basic strength of the conservative movement comes from the middle and lower middle classes. Brophy further described the conservative movement by observing that about 75 per cent of the workers are women—a sort of woman's protest movement like the suffragettes. Women, he said, seem to have more courage and less inhibitions.

As the interview drew to a close and I put my notebook away, Frank Brophy went to a file drawer and produced three rolls of charts "documenting" the "Jewish-Communist Conspiracy" in this country in 1939. While discounting the Jewish role, he nevertheless drew it to my attention.

I asked one final question: Is the Kennedy administration applying any particular pressure on conservative or anti-Communist leaders through special "reviews" or investigations of their income-tax returns? Brophy has heard of no such tactics.

Brophy is not particularly hysterical, paranoid, or suspicious in his manner; he is actually rather calm and restrained in his appraisal of the "Communist menace." In this sense, he is very much like Colonel Bunker.

Meeting with about fifty of the faithful in the private dining room of an ultra-modern motel on the outskirts of Wichita, we had just eaten a cold-cut and salad luncheon for which we had paid five dollars. The luncheon was a distinct disappointment, but the speaker the five dollars was helping to subsidize looked much more promising.

In his introductory remarks, Robert Love, the youngest member of the Council, had a few rather harsh things to say about the apathy of the local members of the Society. It seems they were not out in full force to hear Dr. Draskovich, a Council member, and there was the lurking suspicion that this was because they were asked to help pay the expenses. Bob Love commented that he didn't mind carrying them on his back—it only bothered him when they dragged their feet.

Love introduced Dr. Draskovich as a man who was trying to warn and inform the uninformed. He said that we would agree with him that the opposition is not the problem, but the uninformed who fall for anything.

Draskovich lived up to his introduction—he informed us of a great deal indeed—only we wondered whether we were being properly "informed," for Draskovich lives in a very different world from ours. He opened by saying that before the general public one has to speak cautiously, but among friends he felt free to speak openly.

The situation is bad and getting worse and worse. Since 1944, the Communists have grown from two hundred million to nine hundred million strong. (Where did this figure come from? Does it include in the Communist camp every neutral nation and grant non-Communist status only to Spain, France, and West Germany?) But Draskovich goes on. Castro is only ninety miles from our shores. . . . The current drive of the Communists is toward respectability. . . . Stalin was bad, but Tito and Khrushchev and others are "good" Communists. He goes on to say our foreign policy is clearly subversive when we give aid or co-operation to a Communist country even "when their interests coincide with ours."

Within this country we have to fight not only the anti-anti-Communists, Draskovich warns, we must also be alert to false anti-communism. He scores Goldwater and William F. Buckley, Jr., editor and publisher of *National Review,* for their attacks on Welch. And he decries the anti-Communist training schools such as those of Fred C. Schwarz—the Australian physician, psychiatrist, schoolteacher, Baptist lay preacher and new full-time head of the "Christian Anti-Communist Crusade." Draskovich says such "schools" spend four days talking about nine-foot-tall Communists, and then only one day on two main "answers" to the threat of communism, both of them ineffectual. The answers of Schwarz are (1) "to pray and pray and pray" and (2) to "study, study, study." These, Draskovich thunders, are not enough! We need the John Birch Society. The Birch Society, he tells us, is exceptional. They are better informed and better financed. We're not in an ideological battle, or a beauty contest or a "seminar"; we're in a struggle for the power to defend America and the world against the Communists. The main problem we face is not "creeping socialism," but "galloping treason." And, Draskovich concludes, the John Birch Society *alone* meets all these problems fully.

He tells us that we don't have to know *everything* about communism to fight it. We don't have to know all about Communist theory in order to destroy it, any more than we have to know all about a hyena to shoot him. And he adds the sinister observation that "they" didn't hold back in fighting the Nazis. The tasks for the John Birch Society, Draskovich says, are to keep informed and to keep *moral indignation* in America from becoming diluted intellectualism. We must keep moral indignation alive; we must be the main moral agent of moral revolt.

He admits that the Birch Society and Welch are not perfect, but he says we've had nothing and nobody better since McCarthy. The Birch Society must stay at the helm of the conservative movement and be directed by strong leadership. We're not against other conservative groups, but we *must* retain control. Draskovich makes a final defense of Welch by saying that, since he was never President, or Vice President, or Secretary of State of the United States, he can't be responsible for the mess we're in.

In the questions that follow, Draskovich has some encouragement for those assembled. He says that not only is interest in the Society continuing to develop, but that its leaders and members are also developing. The discussions and the threshing out of problems among the members and the leaders has helped people to grow. Those who were once only privates are now sergeants, lieutenants, even generals, and can influence thousands. You wonder whether Welch wishes there were a few less ambitious generals under his command.

That evening, the faithful of Wichita gathered again, this time in the stone mansion on the estate of Fred Koch. We met, not on the first floor of the home which is perhaps reserved for those whom the Koches consider their social peers, but in the basement trophy room. The room looks practically medieval. Its split-level length is finished in stone and timbers and its walls are crowded with stuffed heads from the disappearing wildlife of Africa and North America. In opening remarks one speaker said that if the Communists ever take over, they will point to this as the place where the Americanist "conspirators" met.

One of the co-ordinators in Wichita added a "progress report" before Draskovich was introduced, commenting that, we've gotten a lot of the "nervous nellies" up to the trough, but we haven't yet gotten them to drink.

Fred Koch introduced the speaker of the evening, again Dr. Draskovich, as formerly a Professor of Sociology and Economics at the University of Belgrade, the capital of Yugoslavia.

Dr. Draskovich repeats his afternoon speech, opening with

the same remark that among friends one can speak openly and adding that the New Frontier is showing its colors quickly enough to make his message more believable. He again scores Goldwater for his "softness on Communism," in saying that about thirty people leading the Americans for Democratic Action are hurting America, *but* that they're sincere and loyal Americans. Draskovich says no! It's treason! He "informs" his hearers that the UN is impossible and immoral and that there is no difference between Stevenson and Gromyko, that they could well be traded. No one is either shocked or surprised.

Draskovich indicts the mass media, pointing out that the movies on TV are always against the Nazis, never against the Communists. The plot he says is obvious. This *was* news, at least to one who had always assumed that these were just old movies.

Robert Love is one of the new members of the Council and, at thirty-eight, its youngest. He is very well-to-do, but is scarcely a self-made man. His father started and owns a business—the Love Box Company—which Robert helps to run when he is not writing and speaking for the Birch Society. The Love Box Company manufactures cardboard boxes in a modern plant and enjoys the benefits of the Kansas Right to Work Law.

I spent some three and a half hours talking with this energetic young man. His office is only of medium size, but otherwise it has all the status symbols of a top executive. In our discussion, a wide range of topics were touched.

Ayn Rand is a fine spokesman for conservatives, provides the best defense for the profit system, and has a very sparkling character, but Bob Love, like many others in the Birch Society, mourns the fact that she's anti-religious.

We have an "upsurge" of conservatism, Love believes, because the average person is beginning to realize that the problem is not any *one* program of federal aid, foreign aid, social security, or graduated income tax, but the cumulative effect. There is never any end to the number of programs liberals can devise to spend other people's money.

Love takes considerable pride in being a "consistent conservative." He criticizes other conservatives who are against all federal aid and controls except when the government supports their own businesses. Many conservatives in the milk business are quite happy with price control, in the wheat business with government subsidy; another favors issuing of government bonds to promote his industry. He believes that many of these inconsistent conservatives are going to wake up confused with what they've taken and bought.

Robert Love enjoys goading liberals who support social security and other welfare legislation by asking if they ever saw anybody starve to death? If they answer yes, he asks them why they didn't do something about it. He illustrates his depth of acquaintance with those who live in poverty, those who might be in need of such governmental assistance, by asserting flatly that medical care for the aged is unnecessary in Wichita because there is nobody in town who needs an operation who isn't taken care of by private parties.

Race relations also are to be taken care of by "consistent" conservatism, to be "forced" toward neither segregation nor intergration. Love illustrates his "awareness" of the strength of forces favoring segregation when he says that any colored family can move anywhere in Wichita it chooses and is "free" to.

The laboring man, too, is "free" to take another job if his wages and working conditions are not to his liking. There is, of course, no need for such men to unionize as long as they possess such "freedom." Workers wanting more pay ought not to resort to "coercion." Men out of work are a Christian responsibility, not a governmental one. He is vague on *how* this Christian responsibility is to be met on any large scale. In short, a "consistent" and individualistic conservatism seems to be a very workable policy—for those, like Love, who *already* possess the social, economic, and political power to achieve their ends unaided.

Robert Love and Fred Koch together led the drive in Kansas to pass the misleadingly titled "Right to Work Law," and now, together, they lead the Birch Society in Wichita. They have tried to combine two distinct kinds of leadership; they have tried to carry both the dynamic personal "charismatic" leadership characteristic of Welch and the executive and administrative leadership ordinarily carried by the paid "organization men" in the Society. But Koch and Love, strangely enough, have found the satisfactions of neither. The union of "dynamic personal" and "organization men" is very "wearing" upon men of such prominence as Koch and Love, for they have to share the psychological satisfactions of "dynamic personal leadership" with others whom they must publicly recognize as superiors (such as Welch) or as equals (such as Draskovich). Further, the ordinary paid "organization men" have the satisfactions of salary and of approval for their efforts by those like-minded persons who are superior to them in the business community. But Koch and Love need and receive no salary, and they need no "approval" from those in the business community since none is their "superior." The drawbacks of such joint leadership by these and other Council members is not immediately apparent to them when they undertake local leadership of the Society, but its "wearing" character becomes increasingly apparent once it has been undertaken.

The retired Chief Justice of the Arizona Supreme Court, M. T. Phelps of Phoenix, Arizona, a Council member, lives in a modest white frame home on the outskirts of Phoenix. Through the prestige of his former position and his continuing leadership of the right wing, he has been described as the "high priest" of conservatism in the "valley of fear," he says, by "Roberts of the Washington *Post.*" Judge Phelps is an old man, but his speech still crackles with the phrases which earned him this title of "high priest." A thin man who was admitted to the Bar some fifty years ago and who served as a judge for thirty-eight years, his consuming passion is constitutional law. Judge Phelps believes that most of all we need a restoration of constitutional government in the United States, a restoration according to the purposes and intentions of our founding fathers. The founding fathers, he says, strictly specified the powers delegated to the national government and implied the powers to carry them out. All else is reserved to the states and to the people. He insists that no government should ever have the right to dictate to the citizen his duties and his limitations.

Judge Phelps is especially fearful of those who see our Constitution as outmoded. He says that the language employed in the Constitution by our forefathers was broad enough and general enough to be entirely adequate for today's conditions, yet he is adamant in his rejection of any flexibility in interpretation!

He is also fearful of the delegation of additional powers to the executive branch. He traces this movement as beginning under President Roosevelt, continued with Truman and Eisenhower and then broadened under Kennedy—with the abrogation of the authority of the legislative to establish tariffs, make treaties, and even set taxes—a movement supported by the judicial branch ever since Roosevelt's attempt to "pack" the Supreme Court. In the fight over steel prices the Judge saw President Kennedy as attempting to move into an unconstitutional and dictatorial position. The Constitution, he believes, is not only being violated, but is being emasculated and ignored. He cites the decision of the Supreme Court calling for the reapportionment of congressional districts as interference with Constitutional authority. And he adds that the School Desegregation decision of 1954 clearly overruled at least three decisions on the exact subject.

His protest is summed up in his pathetic recitation that we are being led away not only from God but also from "the old rugged cross" and the Constitution. A one-time, old-time Methodist, now a staunch member of the Bethany Bible Church, he laments that Methodist seminaries have rejected the immaculate conception and the bodily resurrection. If they're not so, he says, then there's nothing left. Our colleges, he goes on, are saying that the Constitution is passé, that the Bible is passé. In short, the things we've lived for and have been willing to die for are being cast aside like broken toys.

Judge Phelps seems lonely and pathetic. He says people with whom he has talked and before whom he has spoken say that they believe everything he says, but he adds bitterly that they're not willing to spend any money to do something about it. But in the Birch Society he has found a home. He sees it as an organization that stands for the same thing he does—constitutional government. He is a Council member and proud of it.

Judge Phelps has opinions, however, that reach far beyond his concern for constitutional law. He is strongly racist. He believes that there are differences between the races, not only sociological but also biological differences among the red, mongolian, Negro, and white races. He adds that it will be a sorry day in the United

States when the white race becomes a mongrel race and that's what Chief Justice Warren wants. He says he grew up with a Negro boy and that every time he's gone back home, he's tried to seek him out. Does Judge Phelps after all these years still call him "boy"?

Finally Judge Phelps believes that "international bankers," the Rothschilds, have controlled the international economy and its depressions since 1694.

He decries the vicious attacks upon the John Birch Society by the press, which he believes have come because the left-wing press recognizes the Society's influence. And he predicts that, if the smear keeps up, the John Birch Society will grow to a million members within five years.

The Executive Committee

The Council's "Executive Committee" has emerged as a very powerful advisory group. Made up of five members of the Council: William J. Grede of Milwaukee; A. G. Heinsohn, Jr. of Sevierville, Tennessee; Fred C. Koch of Wichita; Clarence Manion of South Bend; and Robert W. Stoddard of Worcester, Massachusetts, this group meets at least once every three months and other interested Council members seem to be free to drop into its meetings.

By November, 1961, this group had succeeded in gaining the right to review and to "approve" the monthly Bulletins written by Welch which contain the "Agenda for the Month" for all the members of the Society. One of the Council members explained to me that the function of the Executive Committee was to "help Bob Welch to maintain the breadth of perspective to keep the Society functioning well" and observed that Welch isn't always able to do all the outside reading necessary and that the Executive Committee appear to have modified the leadership of Robert Welch to a rather substantial degree.

CHAPTER IV

The "Organization Men"

Not only does Welch find his leadership challenged and moderated by his Council members, but there are much subtler modifications which come through the almost continuous contact he has with his "organization men," who serve as administrators in the home office and as co-ordinators of various rank throughout the country.[1] Most of these men are young, and nearly all of them have a keen sense of what is "good for public relations" for themselves, for the Society, and for Welch. Since they must at least occasionally deal directly with an "unconverted" public which they hope to convert, there is an almost continual feed-back to Welch about what he should and should not do or say if he wants to attract anyone else from "out there" into the Society. This feed-back is sometimes couched as tactfully selective praise or "suggestions" and sometimes—reminiscent of Welch's campaigning days for the nomination for Lieutenant Governor—in outright exasperation.

Chief among these "organization men" is the District Governor for the Birch Society in California, Oregon, Washington, Arizona, Nevada, and Idaho, John H. Rousselot. Welch contends that his immediate successor will most likely come from the Council, and among its members the name most mentioned is that of Colonel Bunker. But outside of the Council the name mentioned increasingly as Welch's successor is that of John Rousselot.

Rousselot was one of the two Congressmen who publicly acknowledged their membership in the Birch Society when the Society became front-page news in early 1961. The other was Congressman Hiestand, also of California, who was defeated in the 1962 election.

Rousselot was elected as the state president of the Young Republicans early in his career. Careful observers of California politics describe Rousselot as a real banner carrier in anything he goes in for. And they commented that, although he's a devoted Christian Scientist, they always thought he was the type who would make a good fire-and-hell Baptist preacher. He attracted a strong following of young supporters and workers who helped him get elected to Congress on the extreme right-wing Birch line and they thought that he would stick by it.

As far back as 1961, the conservative Los Angeles columnist, George Todt wrote admiringly of Rousselot in action.[2] He reported: ". . . I listened to a brilliant young . . . Congressman from California—Johnny Rousselot of Arcadia—and his staunch Americanism sent an overflow crowd at the Shakespeare Club in Pasadena into what might be described as an explosion.

"There is a great wave of conservatism sweeping the nation nowadays," Todt continued, "and Rousselot is one of its most articulate junior spokesmen. He is only thirty-two but possesses much political wisdom and savvy. He speaks out like a young California edition of Sen. Barry Goldwater.

". . . After a lovely musical program, Rousselot swung into action—and held the audience spellbound for most of an hour." It seems "He has a particular appeal to youth, but it is by no means limited to any specific age group." Todt predicted ". . . an increasingly useful political future for this hard-hitting young American patriot. He ought to go far. And undoubtedly will do so.

"As a matter of fact, it is hardly less than an open secret that Johnny Rousselot is thinking seriously of trying for the toga of a United States Senator on the 1962 ballot." George Todt went on to outline the desirability of a contest in the Republican primary btween Rousselot and Kuchel, saying that such a primary fight, "if on a high plane—would do much to stir up general interest in the over-all campaign."

When disclosure was first made of Rousselot's affiliation with the Birch Society, he made a real attempt to duck the most damning aspect of this connection. He said at a press conference in April, 1961, and repeated in the *Congressional Record* of February 15, 1962, that he totally disagreed with Welch's contention that Eisenhower was a conscious agent of the Communist conspiracy. Rousselot also said that he personally had had other areas of strong disagreement with Robert Welch, which he made clear not only to the press and to his constituents, but also to Mr. Welch himself. But Rousselot also disagreed with those who thought Welch should resign as leader of the Birch Society just when the conservative anti-Communist movement was beginning to win and just because the members do not agree on every item. But this ploy of agreeing with critics of Welch while still attempting to retain the political support of the members of the Society in his home district apparently won him no new support. Further, the redistricting done by the Democratically controlled California State Legislature gerrymandered away most of his supporters. It reduced the number of John Birch chapters within his district from fifty-nine to five. Quite sure at this point that he would attract no confirmed liberals in his new district, he made an all-out attempt to sell the district on the John Birch Society. On June 12, 1962, he inserted into the *Congressional Record* a widely reprinted statement favoring the Birch Society, consisting of his own ten-point analysis of its beliefs and principles. Rousselot reported that Birch Society members are deeply religious, that they oppose and seek to bury the whole international Communist conspiracy on religious, moral, and political grounds. In addition, Birch Society members use not foul but praiseworthy means in the pursuit of praiseworthy ends; they believe in patriotism; and in the constitutional Republic of our Founding Fathers. Further, the Society is opposed to collectivism in all its forms; favors drastic curtailment of the size and functions of our Federal government; believes in eternal vigilance; holds that history *both* repeats itself *and* is governed by ambitious persons and small groups of persons (such as the Birch Society) ; is in favor of less government, more responsibility, and a better world; and, seeks to raise a standard to which the wise, the honest, and the honorable can repair. Who, besides those favoring motherhood, could ask for more?

Two days later Rousselot again scored in the *Congressional Record* on behalf of the Birch Society. He printed the report of a private investigating firm, the "Efficiency Research Bureau," which was hired by the president of a manufacturing firm in Orange County, California, to make an impartial study of the Birch

Society in that county. Among the fourteen conclusions was the following self-contradictory one: "Utilizing both white and colored investigators, it was learned that the John Birch Society isn't anti-Semitic, anti-Negro or anti any religious group. That they, in fact, have chapters comprised entirely of colored membership. Also, it was found [that the] John Birch Society has Jewish members on the national advisory council."

Turning to a more dramatic approach in his campaign, Rousselot "confessed," in an interview with the press in April, 1961, that he had been a "Communist dupe."[3] "Yes, you can quote me," he added. "I'm willing to stand up before the American people and say I've been deceived by the Communists." He went on to give examples. "When I was in college I was told by my professors, by my textbooks and by the press that Mao Tse-tung was a peasant reformer, that all he wanted to do was free the Chinese workers. But Mao has executed over two hundred million Chinese people. He turned out to be one of the deceitful men of the Communist conspiracy.

"Here's another example of how I was taken in by the press, radio and television coverage of another agrarian reformer—Fidel Castro: Ed Sullivan stood up on his program and put his arm around Fidel and said, 'I want you to meet the George Washington of Cuba.' Again I was taken in. I was deceived.

"Does this mean that Sullivan was a Communist?" Rousselot asked rhetorically. "No," he said with an emphatic shake of his head. "Sullivan was deceived, too. We both were dupes."

Rousselot said that it was easy for Americans to be deceived by the Communists, but defended Welch as a "far-seeing, fine man" whom the Communists have not been able to deceive.

A reporter asked how Rousselot knew that he was not being deceived by Welch. "That's a fair question," Rousselot says. "I know this man. I've met him on two occasions. In fact, I talked with him on the phone just the other day. I suppose he's made mistakes—we all do. But basically he's been right. He's had harsh things to say. I don't agree entirely with him, but he should have a chance to be heard."

Rousselot told the reporters that it was true that some members of the Society had made "irresponsible" charges. "But that doesn't mean that the Society is totally bad, just because there have been some instances of impropriety. It's wrong—at least I think it's wrong," Rousselot added, "to accuse another person of being a Communist without documentation." But it's not always possible to find full documentation because of the "deceitful nature" of communism. We don't always get reasonable documentation, Rousselot said, "because people get emotionally carried away."

However, he concluded that John Birch members are "people of integrity," who feel that they have "the responsibility for exposing the Communist conspiracy in a positive way by speaking up."

Appearing on "Open End" a few days later[4] for a televised debate on the Birch Society, Rousselot displayed his skill in the infighting of debate. Though somewhat burdened by his partner Tom Anderson—a very vocal member of the Council who is always willing to take a flat-footed stand on the end of a limb—Rousselot scored again and again as he chose phrases from his opponents and turned them to his own advantage. Senator McGee, in opposition to the Society, held his own quite well as he insisted that *The Politician* must be considered representative of the Society since it is a statement of the views of its founder. But Dr. Bennett of Union Theological Seminary, the other opponent of the Society, who tried to bring careful statement and rational analysis into the debate, was cut down time after time by Rousselot as he demonstrated the less polite arts of rhetoric, designed not to clarify issues but to decimate an opponent.

As the election drew near, Rousselot chose not to enter the race for Senate against the liberal Republican incumbent Kuchel, but to seek instead re-election in his gerrymandered congressional district. Having moved into a position of full support of the Birch Society, Rousselot ran into determined liberal opposition from the Republican as well as the Democratic parties, for both the Birch Society and their liberal opponents saw the campaign as a crucial test of the political appeal of the extreme right wing.

Rousselot was defeated in the election. But he got the "consolation prize" of another office for the campaign he had run. Robert Welch announced in the December, 1962, *Bulletin* that "John Rousselot will become, on January 1, our District Governor for the six western states of California, Oregon, Washington, Arizona, Nevada, and Idaho. And we are sure that through his speeches, his friendships, and his following, through his energy, his knowledge and his dedication, John will be of tremendous help in rapidly building the strength of the Society west of the Rockies." Rousselot's new office is in San Marino, California, and John told friends in Congress that his new salary was $50,000 a year. The high position and phenomenal salary add substance to the contention of many that John Rousselot has become second only to Robert Welch in the command of the John Birch Society.

In assuming the position of District Governor, Rousselot has displaced Ed Griffin, who had formerly been the top paid executive for the Birch Society in California.

Ed Griffin ranks among the "coolest" organization men employed by the Society. In a very cautious and businesslike forty-five-minute interview in the spring of 1962 this calm, pleasant-appearing young man in his mid-thirties, who was formerly in the insurance business, discussed the strategy of the rising conservative movement. As we sat talking in his well-furnished but unpretentious office in the midddle of Los Angeles, he compared the conservative strategy of recruitment with that of the Communists. The Communist strategy has two steps. First they create in prospective followers a complete disillusionment with the existing social, economic, and political order. When this process of disillusionment is complete, the Communists move to their second step: they fill this void with the utopian dream of communism. The same thing, he says, has begun to happen with the conservatives. The first step has already been taken by many of their prospective followers; a feeling of disenfranchisement and disillusionment has already begun and has only to be completed. The next step for the Birch Society is again parallel—to fill the void with a utopian dream. The strategy of recruitment is the same, but the content of the dream is, of course, different. It is a utopian dream of limited government and a free market or, in the official motto of the Birch Society, "less government, more responsibility and a better world."

The first step in the process is the collapse of trust in the

68   THE JOHN BIRCH SOCIETY

social, economic, political, educational, and religious institutions
of our nation. And Ed Griffin and other Birchers apparently are
sanguine in their conviction that, as this proceeds, they can out-
maneuver the Communists in the ensuing chaos of disillusionment and ensure that the Birch Society's utopian dream, rather
than the Communist utopian dream, will be built upon the ashes
of the old order.

Mr. Griffin's cool logic should give all thoughtful Americans
and even Birch Society sympathizers reason to pause and ponder.

Ed Griffin is a very calm and proper "organization man."
"Butch," the Birch Society co-ordinator for an area that includes
a large city and a major agricultural area, is of quite a different
temperament. Living in a large frame house in the suburbs, he
has converted his third floor into an office. The room is carpeted
and cluttered with stacks of books, pamphlets, and audio-visual
equipment. An American flag is prominently displayed. Butch,
who likes to be called by his nickname, tells me that the room
was redone to give him and his wife a place in which to get away
from their three small kids, and to give the kids a chance to get
away from them.

Butch is a man of about forty, with pale eyes; he is fairly
short and of medium build. After explaining my scholarly interest
in the conservative movement in general, and in the Birch Society
in particular, I showed him my credentials identifying me as a
graduate student of Boston University. After examining them, he
began to tell me about the anti-Communist movement. He
says that the upsurge of conservatism has come particularly in
anticommunism. It has found its growth as people have developed the ability to analyze the actions of the news media. It seems
that attacks upon the Birch Society have cost it some members,
but that the Society has been painted as so bad that a great
many more prospective members become curious.

Butch believes attacks against the Birch Society began in
Moscow in February, 1960. A general attack upon the Society
shifted to an attack upon Welch, and degenerated to character
assassination directed against both Welch and himself. Both Welch
and Butch have been called Fascists, racists, little dictators and
so on.

At that point, Butch fixed me with a pale, narrow-eyed, suspicious gaze, and wheeled around to pick up his phone. "If you don't mind," he said, "I'll just give my major co-ordinator a call." He was unable to reach him and talked with his secretary instead. Yes, she remembers that a graduate student fitting my description had talked with her boss. Butch, his suspicious temporarily allayed, chatted with the secretary for a few moments, hung up, and returned to his conversation with me.

His train of thought brought him to the subject of anonymous phone calls. They are not used by members of the Birch Society, he asserted, but he himself receives an average of about twelve threatening phone calls from "the opposition" in the course of each month.

Butch commented that many politicians are swinging into line with this anti-Communist drive, but he's not positive what their motives are for doing so. He believes that the conservative anti-Communists hold a strong political position because neither party knows whom they will support.

He then spoke of his reaction to the National Council of Churches. It seems he and his family left their Presbyterian Church because of its affiliation with the National Council. And Butch reports that the minister came and talked with them for three hours. He claims that the minister broke down and cried telling him that the National Council of Churches held title to his church and land and that they would defrock him if he tried to lead his congregation out of the National Council.

How do persons become conservatives? Self-study is the basic way, Butch thinks. He told of his own experiences of being introduced to the vast literature purporting to "document" internal subversion. He went through hundreds of books, staying up very late at night for seven months straight to read them. That was enough to convince him! But, he said, you can get almost the same effect by reading "One Dozen Candles," which is a package-deal kit of twelve reprints of books selected and promoted by the Birch Society as primers on the Communist conspiracy. Here are brief outlines of the twelve "candles" in the kit, as described by Robert Welch.

ONE DOZEN CANDLES

"It is better to light one candle than to curse the darkness."

1. *While You Slept,* by John T. Flynn.

    Will show you how so many developments, of huge and tragic significance, could have been brought to pass without your being aware of the forces behind them.

2. *The Web Of Subversion,* by James Burnham.

    With names, dates, and specific facts this book reviews some part of the Communist infiltration into our government itself which had already been exposed, before the executive order of May 17, 1954, issued by President Eisenhower, made further exposures impossible.

3. *America's Retreat From Victory,* by Senator Joseph R. McCarthy.

    Few Americans will believe this book *until they have read it.* But few fail to believe *after* they have read it. The almost incredible but fully documented story of George Catlett Marshall.

4. *Odyssey Of A Fellow Traveler,* by Dr. J. B. Matthews.

    Now we go back two decades, to see how hundreds of "united fronts" were created, manipulated, and used by the Communists to condition the American People to be led by Stalin's agents. Written by a misguided idealist who helped to create these fronts and then, completely disillusioned, did all he could to expose them.

5. *Shanghai Conspiracy,* by Major General Charles A. Willoughby.

    The foundation laid, Stalin uses his worldwide espionage apparatus, as well as propaganda pressures, to bring on World War II, and to get the United States into that war as his ally. General Willoughby, as former Chief of MacArthur's "Intelligence," writes from direct personal knowledge and experience.

6. *From Major Jordan's Diaries,* by George Racey Jordan.

    We are now ready to look again at American power—throughout the greatest war in history and its aftermath—being commandeered by Communists to serve the purposes of Stalin. Here is one tiny but important segment of the whole terrible tableau.

7. *I Saw Poland Betrayed,* by Ambassador Arthur Bliss Lane.

    One use by the Communists of American money, prestige, and productive might was to enable them, within five years after the war was over, to enslave all the countries of Eastern Europe. Here is a case history in that brutal subjugation.

8. *The People's Pottage,* by Garet Garrett.

    In the meantime, the Communist-inspired conversion of Amer-

ica, from a constitutional republic of self-reliant people into an unbridled democracy of handout-seeking whiners, was proceeding according to plan. And still is. Here is the one book that tells the basic
story best.

9. *The Kohler Strike,* by Sylvester Petro.

The ground we are trying to cover in these twelve books is so
vast that we must supply an understanding of whole huge areas by a
detailed picture of just one sample scene. Here in minuscule com-
pleteness is the whole story of the part played by labor bosses, whom
the Communists love, in gradually destroying our great inheritance.

10. *The Pentagon Case,* by Victor J. Fox.

In Poland, in Indonesia, in Bolivia, in many other countries, the
destruction or extreme demoralization of the armed forces of the
nation was a prelude to its final complete capture by the Communists. Here we see—though told as fiction—some aspects of the
deliberate demoralization of our own "services," which demoralization has been carried immensely further since this book was written.
It is enthralling as a novel, but terrifying as history.

11. *The Tragedy Of Bolivia,* by Alberto Ostria Gutierrez.

Another case history, this one showing the now increasingly rapid
and widespread subjugation of Latin America by the Communists,
through the use of our millions and our might for exactly the opposite purpose from what the people of the United States are told
by their government. The Communist takeover of Bolivia having
been completed by 1956, with the United States supplying the means,
this carefully documented record of the tragedy is extremely revealing
as to what is happening almost everywhere else in Latin America
today.

12. *Nine Men Against America,* by Rosalie M. Gordon.

We complete our dozen books with perhaps the most important
on the list. For Rosalie Gordon's thin volume on the Supreme Court
shows how this body under Chief Justice Warren has been destroying
every safeguard which might prevent the Communists from carrying
out their plans. If the American people would just learn and understand what the Supreme Court really has been doing, that alone
would start the necessary revolt against policies which betray us. We
do not hope for so much from one book. But we do hope that this
whole dozen books will supply a mighty push in that direction.

Butch admits that he lost a lot of sleep over these books. He
told me of a retired Admiral who couldn't finish them without

getting sick to his stomach and he added that he doesn't understand how people can fail to be moved when the evidence is right
before them. I recalled to mind the boast of Stalin that paper will
stand anything put upon it—and that the honesty and the accuracy
of any so-called evidence from a document, from a book, or from
a person must be evaluated upon all the additional facts and information available and that this certainly includes evidence *beyond* the assertion of honesty and accuracy by the author of a document, of a book, or of a statement.

Butch's version of how people are recruited into the Birch
Society, differs from that of Ed Griffin only in point of view. Butch
sees four steps in the process. First, informing oneself. The reactions of people during this step lead them through three emotional
stages: alarm, depression, and finally anger. Anger leads to the
second step, informing others—informing one's family, neighbors,
and friends through conversations and letters. Butch notes that
the anti-Communist "schools" of Schwarz, Hargis and "Operation
Alert" are especially helpful in these first two steps. The third
step is the desire to take action against this all-embracing web of
Communist subversion. At this point, Butch notes, one's actions
are most apt to be defensive—protesting something. Finally the
fourth step—the move from defensive to offensive action. One
wants to prevent things from happening. Seeking long-range goals,
one becomes a member of the John Birch Society. He becomes a
member because this Society is the ultimate among the anti-
Communist groups. It is basically an action group, not only a
study group, and this, Butch adds, is why it's been so strongly
attacked.

Butch's wife seems to have joined this fight with him. She
has been very active in her PTA. Recently she attacked a series
of articles on how to fight communism. These articles were brought
to the attention of her PTA and she proceeded to "expose" their
authorship. It seems they were written by Harry Overstreet and,
Butch tells you, he has nine citations against him. The thought
runs through your mind that John Foster Dulles, when he was on
his deathbed, handed President Eisenhower a book co-authored
by this same man and his wife entitled *What You Must Know
About Communism*. With just a little practice one could begin

to think just like a Bircher—that is, you could learn to parlay infinitesimal bits of evidence into a major exposure! But back to Butch's wife. It seems that it's quite all right to mention nine so-called citations against a man, but both Butch and his wife are always careful not to call anyone a Communist. Butch concludes that his wife is probably the least liked person up at the school, but that that doesn't make any difference to her. She knows what's right, and once you know what's right you *have* to stick with it, Butch adds emphatically.

I asked Butch about his work, how many hours a week he puts in, if it was a full-time job? He replied that he puts in about sixty hours a week, but that he gets very little salary. The liberals, it seems, have all the money from the big tax-free foundations. One bad thing about this work, he said, is that you talk over the phone all the time and you get sick and tired of it. It's at least possible that many Birch Society leaders are serving as counseling outlets for thousands of neurotics who would otherwise be appealing to their neighbors, their public servants, or their ministers.

I asked about the chapter meetings he supervises. Are they "all business" or are they also a social outlet? Butch replied that they're basically business, not social. There is perhaps some friendly exchange, but they're there for business.

Suddenly Butch volunteered the information that some people, even some conservatives, are spreading the rumor that he's a Communist infiltrating the John Birch Society. Then he paused and eyed me suspiciously once again. "Who are you anyway?" he muttered half to himself. "You might be a newspaperman. I might see this in the headlines tomorrow." Then another possibility crystalized in his mind, "You know," he said. "You might even be from the Home Office in Belmont."

Getting no response, Butch repeated that he can't understand how people can fail to be moved when the evidence is right before them. He concluded the interview by commenting that he likes to master anything he starts. It seems that he is now determined to "master" his segment of the Birch Society.

Not all of the "co-ordinators" who organize and oversee local chapters are paid. Many of them render their services on a volunteer basis. Mr. and Mrs. Johnson are volunteer co-ordinators. Mr. Johnson is a retired army officer, but he tells you that he and Mrs. Johnson have always worked as a team and they continue this in their work in the Society. Joining the Birch Society with a very deep sense of patriotism, they feel that the Constitution is the greatest document ever written and that, through fidelity to it, ours has become the greatest country in world history. Mr. and Mrs. Johnson are anxious that we reverse what they feel to be attempts to undercut our national heritage by the "one worlders" in our nation and in our government. They see the Council of Foreign Relations and the Institute of Pacific Relations as the most dangerous and active agencies pursuing a one-world government in our country. Concern for our nation's future is deeply personalized for them because of their seven grandchildren. They want to insure that these grandchildren grow up with the same advantages that they had.

The rise of the Birch Society has come, according to them, because the American people have become dissatisfied with the modern trend of government. So many of our tax dollars are used for foreign aid, yet they buy no loyalty to us because the neutrals will align themselves not on the basis of foreign aid but according to which side they think is going to win. As the Johnsons travel about, speaking and showing films, recruiting and organizing Birch Society chapters, they find people more and more concerned wherever they go.

You cannot coexist with the devil, the Johnsons say, and the fight has become one between Christianity and anti-Christ. But, strangely enough, they comment, the churches are actually doing very little in this fight. They see the Christian Church, especially as led by the National Council of Churches, as always coming up on the wrong side of the fight. The National Council, they claim, wants Red China admitted into the United Nations. It wants to abolish the House Committee on Un-American Activities, and it also wants to abolish the Connelly Reservation, which limits the jurisdiction of the World Court over our international relations. Ministers, priests, and rabbis are in a very good position to use their pulpits to help in the fight for God, country and freedom, but they're not helping.

The Johnsons conclude by revealing that they were in a very serious car accident in which both their lives were somehow spared. Consequently they feel that God's purpose for their lives is for them to continue their anti-Communist fight.

The full-time paid co-ordinator for one Southwestern state is Mr. Cooper, a congenial and attractive man in his early fifties with prematurely graying hair. Mr. Cooper is a disarming representative for the Society with nothing of the fanatic in his manner or in the presentation of his views. The growth of interest in the Birch Society has come, he explains, not with any dramatic upsurge, but simply as more and more people have done more studying, and thinking, and talking. The churches, he says, haven't been much help in this growth of concern over communism; neither have the schools. In fact, he adds, many religious and educational leaders have opposed the program of "Planned Patriotism" which has been initiated in many of the school districts of his state. This opposition seems to have come from religious leaders dedicated to the National Council of Churches and united with educational leaders in the American Civil Liberties Union, and the World Federalists. These opponents, Cooper says, also opposed "Operation Abolition," the film purporting to demonstrate the Communist leadership of the student demonstrations turned riot during the hearings of the House Committee on Un-American Activities in San Francisco. Some of these same people have also attacked the conservative press of his state, a press, Cooper grants that has given the John Birch Society fairly favorable coverage.

Mr. Cooper does not consider himself an extremist in any sense, but his record of frustration as a voter is shared by many a conservative: only once since 1932 has he cast his vote for a winning presidential candidate, and that was in 1952 when he voted for Eisenhower for his first term.

The Kennedy administration was something that Cooper couldn't understand and he cited the President's action challenging the steel price increase, the Tractors for Cuba drive to ransom prisoners from the abortive Bay of Pigs invasion, the moves toward disarmament, and the backing of the United Nations in what Cooper called the "rape of Katanga."

He defended Welch's statement on Eisenhower as a personal opinion, but noted that both sides were prone to make use of such statements from their opposition to seek to discredit them, and cited the right-wing attack upon Kennedy for calling the top management in the steel industry S.O.B.'s.

Cooper observed that there are a great many liberals in his state and lamented that they seem completely unable to discuss the issues that he sees facing our country. It's not that they're reluctant to discuss them, they just seem honestly unable to do so.

Quoting Welch, Cooper says that the thing the Communists fear mostly, especially the ten thousand members of the Communist Party in America, is that the American people will wake up before it's too late.

Concluding our conversation, Cooper maintained that the "exposure" of the Birch Society by the press hasn't lost them many members, but he admits that it may have slowed up the recruiting of new members.

A co-ordinator in the Midwest feels that at the root of the growth of the Birch Society is simply a gradually growing awareness of the peril which Western civilization faces and this is the reason why the position of the Western world has declined so precipitously since 1945. The growth of the Society has been further fostered, he feels, by an increasing concern over the decline in morality, the rise of crime, and increasing mental illness.

Mr. Reynolds is a lawyer who holds his B.A. from Harvard College. He served in the army of occupation in Germany, where he met his attractive and highly intelligent German wife, Helga. His law practice seems to take little of his time and is operated from the cellar of a private home. He seems to derive some income from distributing janitorial supplies, but his home, like his office, indicates a very marginal income. He may get some income from serving as co-ordinator for the Birch Society, but there is also the possibility that he gets no income for this service.

He began to tell me how the Reds moved in and took over Harvard College.

The inside story of the Red takeover of Harvard is available to anyone who has, according to Reynolds, enough Americanism left to look it up. You can't find it in the press. *Keynes at Harvard,* published by the Veritas Foundation, is recommended as a true account of a continuing campaign to "brainwash" the entire academic community of this country into accepting and promoting Fabian socialism which will, in turn serve as a steppingstone to communism.

Reynolds finds the upsurge of interest in conservatism centered upon a return to fundamental religious and moral values, over against what he feels to be the relativity of modernism. In this connection he cites the book by Pitirim A. Sorokin, *The Crisis of Our Age.* He says that this is the best book on the sweep of the problem—the economics in the book are no good, he says, but the thesis is good—that a moral crisis has afflicted every civilization. Sorokin's analysis, Reynolds claims, is even better than Toynbee's.

Another basic problem seen by Reynolds is that the average individual has a basic respect for truth, but doesn't know what it is. Reynolds and the Birch Society seem quite prepared to come to the rescue of such people. He sees the work of the Society as a salting operation, and adds that it doesn't take much to change the flavor.

Among the various right-wing anti-Communist groups, he views the Birch Society as the most cohesive and as having the most esprit de corps. He sees it as a Society of readers. The more they read and research, the more effective and eloquent they are. Further, Reynolds has never met a person who wasn't converted after having completed a number of the books recommended by the Society and tells of one woman who got halfway through a stack of these books and got hives.

Becoming more reflective, he says that there have been three mass assaults on the American mind designed to serve and help communism. The first was to paint Mao Tse-Tung as true democrat and as an antidictatorial agrarian reformer. The second was to attempt the same for Castro with *Christian Century, Look, Life,* Jack Paar, and Drew Pearson and others leading the assault. The third is the new drive against the anti-Communist movement—trying to equate George Lincoln Rockwell, the leader of the American Nazi Party, with the movement—and this assault

has enlisted the co-operation of the government and news media
and the whole leftist group. He says that the mass media in
Germany could have attacked—and almost decided to attack and
destroy—Hitler, but that too many businessmen had already been
bought with Federal aid.

In another city the co-ordinator with whom I talked was Mr.
Davis, a mild young man of about thirty, who along with his
duties as co-ordinator still found time to sell insurance. In his
pleasant tract home in suburbia he described a group which origi-
nated as a protest over training of Yugoslav pilots by the United
States Government as a perfect example of a Birch Society front
organization. The head of it, Davis told me, was a member of the
Birch Society who resigned when he assumed these new duties
so that he could say, when asked, that he wasn't a member. Davis
also indicated that many of its local supporters were members of
the Society. He himself stopped going to their meetings to help
keep them clear of such identification.

Davis was quite proud of one feather in his cap. He had
been on the platform at a meeting at which Welch had spoken.
He described the meeting as an illustration of the attempt of the
press to smear the Society. It seems that this was to be a private
meeting by invitation only, with no representatives of the press to
be admitted. Upon the insistence of the press they were admitted
under the conditions that they were to have only fifteen minutes
before the meeting began to ask questions and to use their
cameras. Welch had the press on the front row. The pictures and
questions were disposed of and the meeting got under way. The
place was reportedly packed with all of its 3,000 seats taken. Welch
completed his address and Davis rose to make a concluding announcement. But right then the members of the press interrupted
and began to bombard Welch with additional questions. In the
ensuing confusion, Davis reported, a correspondent for CBS was
thrown bodily off the stage by an overactive co-ordinator from out
of town. The press, Davis said, made a great deal of this incident,
even though one local paper admitted that the reporters had violated their agreement by asking questions at the end of the
program. It seems that the press is acceptable to Welch and to the

Society only when it "knows its place."

Mr. Davis said he joined the Society because of his three little girls. He wants the same freedom for them that he enjoyed, and this freedom is threatened because the world, he says, is closing in on us; there is a sustained drive to surrender the sovereignty of our country and we need to do something. He sees disarmament, "land reform" under Secretary of Agriculture Orville Freeman, and "socialized medicine" as the greatest threats. He's not a doctor or a farmer, he says, but they have rights which must be protected. If the moral barricade is lost for them, he asserts, it's lost for all.

As a Korean War veteran, he saw our government acting within what he thought were insane limits. He saw the Chinese Communists building up across the Yalu River and our forces were not allowed to attack them. General Walker was there, too, he adds.

When Davis returned from Korea and was attending college, the late Senator McCarthy was at the height of his power. Davis was most favorably impressed by him. But many were appalled and angered over the people McCarthy smeared. Davis said he kept asking for names of people who had actually been smeared. He said he could never get an answer about anyone who had been. At this same time, Bill says, there was a move at his college to get rid of two professors—and the issue of academic freedom was very much in question. But now, it seems, eight or ten years later, there's a bill in the California Legislature to bar professors who are members of the Birch Society from the State University system. Academic freedom is a two-way street, Davis says emphatically.

Mr. Davis mentioned that one of the current projects of the Society is to get Communist-made goods out of stores, since anything that builds up a Communist economy supports a slave system. He bemoans our policy of foreign aid, which he says demands free elections for the dictators we support, but not for the Communists.

As I left, he showed me a room just off the living room, piled high with audio-visual equipment, pamphlets, books, and Walker campaign posters. They had wanted him to help in General

Walker's primary gubernatorial campaign, he says, but he was too busy and this would tie Walker in too much with the John Birch Society.

In the home office in Belmont, Mr. McKinney is the young man who meets you at the door. He is a man well schooled in the arts of public relations, who takes visitors on tours of the home office and who can remember their names, pronunications and all, when he bids them farewell.

Richard Ober is another staff man at the home office. He is in his mid-twenties, married, and with his sharp dress and crew cut looks very much like a recent Harvard graduate—which he is. Dick Ober is the new Business Manager for Welch's *American Opinion*. He has done very well in getting advertisements for this monthly magazine and its readership is growing rapidly especially since the inclusion of Westbrook Pegler and others as regular columnists.

On two occasions I have had the opportunity to talk with Dick at some length—he is an articulate and committed member of the Society—and unlike many of its members with whom I've talked, I get the impression that he's almost listening when I raise issues of disagreement with the analyses and program of the Society. But to the objections and issues that I have raised with him Dick has replied, "If I'm right, then I can either help save my country or I'm already too late to do anything—but if I'm wrong. . . ." I would maintain that intelligent and well-educated people cannot so easily dodge the questions of truth and of means raised by the Birch Society. It is ducking the question to invoke the judgment of history upon questions for which there is already ample evidence. And when such people join any group which in my opinion, divides and weakens our country by destroying faith in its leaders and its basic institutions, I am not at all sure that they can excuse their participation by a belated "discovery" that they were "mistaken." This is doubly true when the evidence they "discover" has been there all the time.

Robert Welch finds himself beleaguered by "advisors" from whom he can find no escape. The council members and his organization men are vitally concerned about what he says and does and at the home office in Belmont or wherever he travels he hears their tactfully oblique, their urgent, and their exasperated words of counsel. Council members have put their influence and reputation on the line in support of Welch and they have no intention of allowing him to abuse this trust.

The organization men are in an even more exposed position. They have to try to recruit from, and answer to, the general public. And day-to-day contact with the public, trying to "justify" and "explain" Welch and the Society, has made them acutely aware of what public relations "image" will "sell." Career considerations are also a concern to those organization men. They want the Birch Society to continue to exist and to grow if only for their own job security, but they are faced with possible necessity of a rapid abandonment of the ship if it appears to be sinking. The captain can go down with the ship if he so chooses, but most of the organization men with families to support cannot afford that luxury of heroism.

And so we see Robert Welch, the "undisputed head" of the John Birch Society, being captured, and his "dynamic personal leadership" being domesticated, by the organization that he himself has created.

CHAPTER V

Chapters or Cells?

Robert Welch seeks to get down to the grass roots, to inform and to arouse the citizenry. To do this he has had to make the leap that has been fatal to many another self-styled leader of the people. He has had, finally, to leap down from his vast organizational superstructure and try to enlist members. These members are supposed to be organized into local chapters. They are to be loyal followers, their loyalty and dedication being given to Robert Welch, the "dynamic personal leader" of the John Birch Society. Organized into local chapters, they are to be the backbone of the Society.[1]

What are chapter meetings like? What goes on? Who shows up for them? The interest in the answers to these questions has been heightened because of the secrecy shrouding the names and the total numbers of the members. One man, a reporter for the Arizona *Journal* of Phoenix decided to try to join and find out. Bud Lanker reported[2] in the spring of 1962 that regular meetings were held at the home of R. Jim Leader. He and his wife, Charlotte, both of whom appear to be in their early thirties, live in a comfortable home on the side of a mountain. It is adjacent to the ten acres and home owned by Mr. Sewell, a retired naval commander, a volunteer state co-ordinator for the Society, and the father of Mrs. Leader.

The Leaders have three small children, a parakeet, and a dog. According to Bud Lanker, they are as pleasant a couple as you would care to meet.

Both Leader and his wife appear to be of above ordinary intelligence, as did most of the persons, both visitors and Society members, who attended chapter meetings at their home. Leader is active in the operation of the Society, but his wife conducted the meetings and referred to herself as the chapter's "leader."

Lanker attended his first meeting February ninth. Present besides him and the Leaders were two other couples. Not much of a turnout, he thought. Later he learned that only three of the other four persons belonged to the chapter. Lanker had been told by Mrs. Leader, when he was invited to attend the meeting, that "several other new members" would be present. He found out later that there were supposedly seventeen members in the chapter, but there were never more than eight out for a monthly meeting.

The meetings never started on time, Lanker relates. The early arrivals sat in the Leaders' family room and chatted about trifles. Mrs. Leader would glance hopefully out the window, prospecting for a large attendance. "I expect———to show up soon," she would say. Or "I hope———will come tonight." She seemed disappointed at the small attendance.

Eventually either she or someone would suggest casually, "Well, I guess we'd better not wait any longer. We might as well get started."

What followed bore little resemblance to an organized meeting, according to Lanker. No roll call was taken. The meetings never were formally called to order. Mrs. Leader appointed one member to lead the group in prayer, after which they remained standing and pledged allegiance to the flag. There always was a large American flag standing in a heavy metal base in a prominent place near a bookcase in the room in which they met. It appeared to Lanker to be a combination family and living room.

Mrs. Leader sat at a large round table covered with books, pamphlets, letters, and leaflets. A tape recorder, on which tapes of anti-Communist dissertations could be played, was in front of her. Members sat in chairs or on a divan. Mrs. Leader dominated the discussion. Much of it was taken up with her reading from Welch's monthly *Bulletin* which each member had received shortly after the first of the month.

While regular meetings were held monthly, Lanker's chapter met at other times to listen to tape recordings or watch films.

At regular meetings, each member was handed an envelope for his monthly report. They were, according to Lanker, supposed to fill out on a form the list of "assignments" they had completed.

That meant the books and periodicals they had read, the public-affairs meetings they had attended, and "additional work done on outside suggested assignments" during the month.

As sort of an "extra," Lanker's chapter had a rubber stamp to use on correspondence. It read: "Don't disarm today, you'll die tomorrow! Don't be the tool for UN one-world rule."

They also received one month a "member's monthly message." This proved to be a lengthy story about Society finances. From it, Lanker gathered the Birch Society could use cash. The message urged members to make "voluntary but regular monthly contributions . . . in addition to their dues." Dues are $2 for men and $1 for women. Why the distinction, Lanker didn't know. Contributions, the message added, were to go directly to John Birch headquarters in Belmont, Massachusetts. These contributions were to be sealed in an envelope and collected at chapter meetings. According to Welch, no one but he "and one or more assistants in Belmont will know who is not making a contribution, who is, or how much."

The meetings, according to Lanker, break up just as they start, following no pattern. Mrs. Leader says, "Well, I guess that's about all." Coffee and the cake are served and members continue to visit informally until they leave.

Meetings of the John Birch Society chapter to which Bud Lanker belonged lasted from two to two and one-half hours. One varied little from the other. He found the proceedings just plain dull. They were one-sided, with Mrs. Leader monopolizing the discussion. Few questions were asked. Most of those present, says Lanker, sat like bumps on a log while Mrs. Leader did all the talking.

Bud Lanker just couldn't figure out what all this had to do with fighting our foe, the Communists. He pressed for an answer from Mr. Leader. At first, Lanker says, he was moderate. He just said he wanted to know how he could take a more active role in pushing the cause. Mr. Leader explained patiently that he *was* fighting the enemy just by attending meetings. He was told to keep reading the monthly *Bulletins* by Robert Welch and follow the instructions.

As far as Lanker could figure out from the *Bulletins,* each

Bircher was expected to conduct a massive one-man letter-writing campaign, directed at our congressmen, state senators and representatives and other public officials. Personal and telephone contacts also were suggested in the *Bulletin*. But neither Mrs. Leader, her husband or any of the other members themselves ever personally suggested to Lanker that he undertake any such campaigns.

Lanker said that one of the things that really "bugged" him was the fact that, from the time he entered the Society until he withdrew his membership, nobody asked him a thing about his background or his occupation—nothing beyond name, address, and telephone number. And, so far as Lanker could determine, the Birch Society screens none of its candidates for membership. Because it was so simple for Lanker to join the Birch Society, a recurring question has nagged at him: Wouldn't it be easy for a Communist to join? And wouldn't super-patriotism be an ideal disguise for an undercover Red? Lanker thinks so. This possibility also finds support in the dark recesses of the logic of Robert Welch—in what he calls "the principle of reversal": those who seem *least* like Communists, for example, really *are* Communists.

Bud Lanker appeared most appalled by the dullness of the meetings and the purposelessness of the activity. And yet his observations of a chapter in Phoenix may well be quite typical. As I have heard leaders and members speak of chapter meetings, and as I have had opportunity to attend them myself, there is the same deadly routine of a movie or a filmstrip or a tape recording for a part of the meeting. And if you've ever tried to sit with a group and listen to *anything* on a tape recorder you have some idea of how deadly this can be. Everyone usually ends up half-hypnotized from watching the reels go around and around and around. . . . After the awful audio-visual—which, for the new recruit, includes a four-reel, two-hour film of Welch—there is always the inevitable "reading" and "commentary" upon the new monthly *Bulletin*.

Mr. Tanner, a "section leader" who supervises several chapters had a number of things to say about their work. A tall, thin man in his middle forties, his congenial low-pressure appeal is perhaps best summed up in his own words: in recruiting he wants prospective members to "buy"; he doesn't want to try to "sell" them on the Society. The long-range program for the Birch So-

ciety Chapters has to do with such items as impeachment, the
State Department, the UN, and income tax. But the more immediate work of a chapter meeting is to check with the *Bulletin* to
see what letters are to be written, to have each member report on
what he did, to collect dues, and to record attendance. Letter-
writing, he says, which makes up a great portion of the activity
of a Society member is about 70 per cent commendatory. Letters of
commendation are much more effective, Tanner feels, than letters
of protest.

He grants that the Society does use many Communistic
tactics, but none, he hastens to add, that are unconstitutional or
unlawful. For instance, Mr. Tanner says, if you're trying to infiltrate a PTA, you can't do it openly. Or, again, if you're against
public health programs, you can't campaign against them. First you
have to gain an office or a position from which to work. But here
he raises the caution that anything a member of the Society
chooses to do outside the monthly agenda in the *Bulletin* has to
be done as an individual and not as a Bircher.

Tanner reports that some of the chapters with which he
works are studying the Constitution, looking for the reasoning
behind the mechanics. But his own particular chapter is studying
clichés of liberals and is learning the arguments against them.
Liberals, he believes, run on clichés and undercutting them is easy
because they don't have the answers. Besides it's fun to watch
them squirm.

Going back to a discussion of the problems of leading a
chapter, he says that you have to keep to the agenda; you can't
get off on something like anti-Semitism, for instance. Further, in
actually working with a chapter, you come to realize that some
people are like sheep. They have to be told, step by step, what
to do.

The collection of monthly dues seems to be the point at
which a check is kept of "live" membership. A member can stop
paying dues and drop out, or a chapter leader can refuse to accept
the dues of a troublesome member and thus force him out of the
Society. The reports by members on what they've done each month
serve as a further check. If a member or a chapter fails to do at
least 50 per cent of the agenda items in the monthly *Bulletins,*

then there is something wrong; an evaluation needs to be made.

The effect of publicity about the Society, the "smear," has been both bad and good, according to Tanner. On the one hand, many conservative people agree with the Birch Society, but don't want to risk the "smear." On the other hand, the "smears" have produced a noticeable net increase in membership, because they have been overdone and have actually served to make people mad.

Speaking of the electorate, following his comments about the sheeplike characteristics of some members, he claimed that anyone can control thirty or forty votes if he prepares. Most of the electorate are a great middle-mass controlled by one side or the other. The Democrats know this and keep their political organization going all the time, but the Republicans do not. This is one of the strong points of the Birch Society, for it is not an organization, but a body like the Roman Catholic Church and this is its strength. He grants that the Society is a "totalitarian" organization, but says that this isn't bad. It means, he says, according to the dictionary, that it has one goal. Tanner notes, however, that the "totalitarian" leadership of Welch is modified by the Council, which has to agree on agenda items. Welch alone is not enough. He indicates that the Council probably does have a successor picked for Welch.

The Chapter Leaders

The chapter leaders are a vital link in the organization of the Society. They have the task of continually trying to arouse and recruit members, of trying to channel the fervor of those already aroused into regular chapter membership, and of directing their pursuit of the national agenda items and of whatever local "projects" the chapter decides to undertake. The chapter leaders, who have these extensive responsibilities, are unpaid volunteers.

Mrs. Miller, a chapter leader, organized one of the first chapters of the Society in California, and has helped to organize at least four other chapters in her area. An active, persuasive, pleasant woman in her forties, she has two sons who have also developed strong interests in the Birch Society. The older one is a sophomore in college. Mrs. Miller has also retained an active part in the California State Republican Party.

Her concern for the growth of what she sees as communism started back in 1956. Her town, she says, became the testing ground for progressive education. Its superintendent even went in for "forced integration." It finally got so bad that the House Committee on Un-American Activities had to be brought in. Starting with this, she began to organize discussion clubs, which were designed to inform their members. These were just study groups; there was no group action, only action by individuals, but this seemed inadequate to many of its members and they organized themselves into patriotic protest groups. This organization now includes hundreds of members whose main activity is to loose simultaneous bombardments of letters to their congressmen or other public officials. They have also been active in circulating petitions for the impeachment of Warren, a long-time project of the Birch Society.

While already deeply involved leading this "protest," Mrs. Miller attended a study seminar led by Robert Welch at the Statler Hilton, held on the same day that Khrushchev arrived in Los Angeles during his visit to the United States. Mrs. Miller was deeply impressed by the national scope of the program outlined by Welch and she proceeded to organize the first chapter in her town, made up completely of women; the other four she organized included both men and women.

Mrs. Miller was deeply disturbed by a series of articles on the Birch Society done by Gene Blake for the Los Angeles *Times* in the spring of 1961. This series was followed by an editorial by the publisher, Otis Chandler, which concluded as follows:

If the John Birchers follow the program of their leader, they will bring our institutions into question exactly as the Communists try to do. They will sow distrust, and aggravate disputes, and they will weaken the very strong case for conservatism.

What are we to think when our last three Presidents, Roosevelt, Truman, and Eisenhower, are accused either of being Communist or Communist dupes?

What are we to think when these charges are leveled against Secretary of State John Foster Dulles, against his brother Allen who heads our vital Central Intelligence Agency, against the Chief Justice of our Supreme Court?

What are we to think when the honor and integrity of the Vice President of the United States, the Republican Party's nominee for President, are questioned?

What are we to think when we are told that our Nation's press almost without exception is Communist infiltrated and inspired?

What are we to think when we are told that our churches almost without exception are corroded with active agents of Moscow?

What is happening to us when all loyal Americans are accused of being Communist dupes unless they subscribe to radical and dictatorial direction of one self-chosen man?

All sincere conservatives must ask themselves the questions. And they must answer them.

The *Times* believes implicitly in the conservative philosophy. It has challenged all these men and most of these institutions on the soundness of one or more issues. But the *Times* does not believe that the argument for conservatism can be won—and we do believe it can be won—by smearing as enemies and traitors those with whom we sometimes disagree.

Subversion, whether of the left or the right, is still subversion.[3]

Mrs. Miller says that this stand by the Los Angeles *Times* has slowed up the growth in membership for the Society; that people will still do the work of the Society, but they won't join. She feels, however, that people are nevertheless deeply concerned. The days of business as usual, and of housewives just staying home are at an end. We are working on survival, people are really sincere, no longer content with the cocktail and golf routine. But she adds that one has to keep a sense of humor or lose effectiveness.

Another chapter in this area meets at the home of its leader, Mr. Parker. He is a slight, thin-faced, rather nervous man in his late thirties. His wife is a pleasant-looking blonde about thirty-five years old. They have six children who watch TV in another room during chapter meetings.

This particular meeting was designed especially for recruit-

ment. I was the first to arrive at 7:45. The meeting, supposed to
start at 7:30, finally got under way at 8:20.

Mrs. Parker was disappointed at the relatively small turnout. She had had good responses from a number of people over
the phone, but none of them showed up. Others who did attend
this recruitment meeting were Ida, Sam, Igor, a Society supervisor
named Harry, and a fat old man. Ida was a pleasant but
lonely old woman of about sixty. She had tried to bring some of
her friends from the drugstore to see the recruitment film. This
seemed to be her first meeting, but she had already written the
home office in Belmont for materials. Ida asked some questions
about Welch's widely quoted statement on Eisenhower and about
the growth of the Society. She was eager to sign the petition which
was passed around for the impeachment of Warren. Sam was a
machine-tool operator of about forty-five, who seemed interested
in joining the Society. Igor, a huge hulk of a man of about
thirty-five or forty, asked a couple of hostile questions regarding
the organizational structure and aims of the Society as compared
to those of the Communists. Igor seemed unimpressed by both
the film and the rest of the meeting. I don't remember the name
of the fat old man, but I do remember that he said he owned
some rental housing and that he was very preoccupied with welfare recipients who didn't pay their rent. This seemed to strike
him as unpatriotic.

After we had sat around talking for a while, the meeting
finally began. Harry, who was introduced as a Birch Society
supervisor—evidently some sort of West Coast assistant to a co-
ordinator—made a few opening remarks and then proceeded to
show us the complete, two-hour, four full 16-mm. reels of the recruitment film. These reels were an unrelieved dose of the "dynamic personal leader," the founder of the John Birch Society,
Robert Welch. In the first three reels Welch dealt with the "Communist menace" mostly at home, but also abroad. He outlined the
international gains of communism, as he saw them, but without
benefit of any visual aids such as a map. He simply peered alter-
nately into the camera and at his notes for the full four reels.
One of the things I remembered most vividly was his rather
rural habit of clearing his throat and then spitting into his hand-

kerchief. Were these excursions into personal hygiene purposely
uncut so as to give the viewer the full impact of his personality?

The changing of the reels was the only break in this presentation. During these breaks we were not invited to get up and
stretch, so the only thing we could do was to gaze bleary-eyed at
one another and agree to both "Isn't this awful?" and "Isn't this
wonderful?" After the outline of the Communist menace in the
first three reels, Welch came through in the fourth reel with the
solution. The answer, it seems, is Robert Welch and the John
Birch Society. Welch recited the same statements he made in the
Blue Book about the need for his dynamic personal leadership,
that the John Birch Society was to last for hundreds of years, that
he wishes no other distinction than to have been its founder, that
it's to be a monolithic organization, that it's the most efficient anti-
Communist group, and that its aims of less governnment and
more responsibility will lead us to a better world.

Harry, the Birch Society supervisor, took it from there. Apparently not wanting to break the mood, he still allowed us no
opportunity to stretch and went directly into a "hard sell." He
dwelt most strongly on the superiority of the Birch Society to other
right-wing groups. He told us that if we were really interested in
counting for something, we should join. He added that the strongest evidence for the effectiveness of the Society was to be seen in
the attack upon it. This "evidence" of the Society's "effectiveness"
has been presented fairly routinely by its leaders and it has always struck me as a little peculiar. Most organizations take time to
evaluate criticisms, rather than viewing all of them simply as
yelps of pain from the "enemy." Certainly a critical editorial from
the conservative Los Angeles *Times* should not be so lightly dismissed. Harry concluded his pitch by pointing up once more the
strong points of the Society: the personal leadership of Welch;
the Society is a "body," not an organization; and finally, the
"long-range" and "basic" program of the Society. Harry hoped we
would all join. With this, the formal part of this recruitment meeting adjourned, and Mrs. Parker graciously served us coffee and
cake. We were given an opportunity to affirm our patriotism by
signing the petition for the impeachment of Warren, and we stood
around (none of us at that point were willing to sit any longer)

and talked. Ida felt equipped now to convince her friends at the drugstore to join the Birch Society. At least she would try.

The Parkers' home, perched on the hillside along a narrow, winding street was a very pleasant place to meet, and the following week I was allowed to attend a regular chapter meeting there. Ida was back and was apparently the only one who had been immediately "recruited." There were five other regular members besides the Parkers in attendance. The meeting followed what is apparently the standard format—a late start; the pledge to the flag; a few opening comments by Mrs. Parker, who then proceeded to read to us the monthly *Bulletin* (which each had received in the mail from Belmont and was supposed to have read before the meeting) ; a review of the current month's agenda set forth by the *Bulletin;* the filling out of reports by members of their performance on last month's agenda; and finally coffee and cake. As we started to depart, it turned out that Ida had no car, so I gave her a ride home. She lived in a very makeshift converted garage. I hope she has found some new friends and some companionship in the Birch Society. But if friendship and companionship were not open to her in a church or civic organization, it is tragic that this spritely but lonely old woman had to turn to a drugstore and to the Birch Society to find it.

Neal is a chapter leader in the Midwest. He is a very ambitious and energetic young businessman who owns a chain of drive-in hamburger stands, now numbering three. He is curly-haired, slender, about twenty-eight, happily married and as deeply dedicated to the Birch Society as he is to the sale of nineteen-cent hamburgers.

Neal sees himself and the Birch Society as moving with, even leading, the tides of history. He believes that the last generation in this country tried socialism (though, he says, they chose to call it liberalism), which was seen as the wave of the future by the young men of Neal's father's generation. But now, he says, people are beginning to take stock. His generation doesn't believe that liberalism was all it was cracked up to be. Neal looks at the Communists moving all over the world, at the devaluation of the dollar, at our basic economic problems, and at our unemployment.

He believes that we need to move back to free enterprise to stimulate our economy, and he equates free enterprise with individual rights.

Neal sees the Birch Society, not as a "reaction" but as a leader in a new and needed shift in direction for our country. This, he says, is why we have the conservative and anti-Communist movements; they are both alike and both spring from the same source of discontent. People often become conservatives through anticommunism, or vice versa. He says that he had been an anti-Communist for seven or eight years and when the John Birch Society came along, it was a natural. The United States is the last free-enterprise and conservative country left. The only other country close to being anti-Communist, he believes, is West Germany, and it is beginning to shift to the left because of pressure from the United States Government. The Communist conspiracy of the last forty years has brought this about, according to Neal.

He and I had our conversation over Cokes in a booth of a beer parlor a few doors down from one of his hamburger stands. He commented rather contemptuously as we left that if people spent as much time reading anti-Communist books as they spent drinking beer, we would be O.K.

One of the more notable regular members of the Society is Greta Olsen, who was born and reared in Germany. At the end of World War II, she was employed by the Allied Occupation Forces and met an American army officer whom she married. Later they came to the United States, where Greta has taught occasional college courses in European history. This work has been on a parttime basis since she is also the mother of three children. She is a brilliant and charming person. She was deeply concerned over the Nazi Government in Germany. She said she was, for instance, the only one in her high school who had read *Mein Kampf,* Hitler's statement of philosophy and personal aims, which has been compared by some to Welch's *Blue Book.*

When she and her husband came to the United States, Greta began speaking on the topic "The Strength of Democracy." She believes that democracy is much better than either Nazism or communism, which are very much alike in their totalitarianism. When they arrived here in 1948, Greta says, the Hiss case was just breaking. She gained the impression that the facts in the case were given in the *Congressional Record,* but not in the general press. Then, she says, McCarthy came along. This was greatly disturbing to her, but since she wanted to make friends in the local college community, which was very hostile to McCarthy, she kept her concerns to herself.

But then, in February of 1960, her husband came home with a copy of the *Blue Book.* Greta read it straight through twice. After just a few pages, she felt that she was seeing the development of Communist power and domination in context for the first time. She had a similar experience later when looking at and showing to others the film *Communism on the Map.* Its impact was overwhelming. It struck her as the truth. The *Blue Book* might have been too staggering for some to accept, but Greta had been prepared for it.

At first she had some qualms about Welch's leadership. She used to joke about his being a fuehrer, but she felt she could easily pull out of the Society if he proved to be such a man. Then she asked herself: What means, after all, does Welch have to make me do what he wants to do except persuasion? She finds herself in agreement with him about 75 per cent of the time, and this, she feels is plenty.

Another experience was added to her reading of Welch's *Blue Book.* This was what she describes as a genuine Christian conversion. This, she says, has given her and other conservatives, who had been very timid people before, a new courage. It was for her a deeply personal experience far more basic than politics.

She reports that her Christian conversion came in July, 1960, just two months after she had joined the Birch Society. She had begun the right-wing books "documenting" Communist subversion. After reading a number of them, she felt way down that we're already lost. She adds that most conservatives feel that maybe we won't win. But she thinks that we have to fight even if we may lose. A "confronted conservative" really has only two choices: to close his eyes and not to fight or to commit himself to it with the help of a personal God. She says that this, for her, means the personal love of God in Christ. She finds that prayer helps—not just fooling her-self, not just self-hypnosis, but finding real help from outside in what she's doing. This has shifted her point of reference from conservatism to fundamentalism. Interestingly enough, she says, it keeps her from any loss of kinship with liberals because they're wrestling with these same issues. The emphasis on fundamentalism, she feels, keeps conservatives from working on preconceived ideas; their only preconception is that we must work by absolute truths as we discover them.

As she talked with me, she added one other point—that we must have compassion for others. She decried what she called the liberal view that the Chinese need to make their peace with history. "In the name of what do they say these things?" she im-plored. There was "peace" in a concentration camp in Germany. Peace at any price of human suffering is not right, she insists; we must resist this with all we have. Because of this, Greta says, she has been called a warmonger. But she saw the war in Germany and it was worth it to get rid of Hitler. If the choice is an evil peace or war, we have to resist evil even if it means war.

This kind of stance points up a real blind spot in a great deal of the "tough talk" of the Birch Society. Their conception of war-fare does not yet include a realization of the basic change in the character of warfare brought about by the development of nuclear weapons. Up till now the basic question of warfare has always been: Are some men so evil that they must be destroyed? The question before us now in nuclear warfare is: Are some men so evil that all men must be destroyed? Until the tough-talking leaders and members of the Birch Society face this fact their sword-rattling deserves little attention.

Mr. Batsford is a notable member of the Society in the Midwest. He is a voluble person in his early thirties with four small children and a wife who is very much opposed to his par-ticipation in the Society. He is a persistent writer of letters to the editor and often gets his views in print. As soon as I came in the door, he greeted me warmly and offered me a bourbon. I muttered something about being a Methodist minister and declined. When his wife heard that I was going to talk with her husband about the Birch Society, she wanted nothing to do with it and departed to visit a neighbor.

According to Batsford, the current members of the Society were already conservatives and when the John Birch Society came along, it was a natural for many of them as it was for him. But he noted rather sadly that membership in the Society had alienated some members from their former friends. He mentioned the charge of fascism against the Society. He said that Welch is definitely not a Fascist; that, on the contrary, he's a mild-mannered, nervous type of individual; that it's hilarious to think of him as a "man on horseback," and he added that he wouldn't support Welch if he was. Furthermore, if the Society ever did take a Fascist shift, its members would depart.

It's sad, he says, that we need a John Birch Society. We wouldn't need it if we could get our views over, but the mass media, he feels, are overwhelmingly liberal. The Birch Society has hurt the Communists and the liberals, he believes, by slowing up people and encouraging them to think. People have had to be shaken up and shocked by the Birch Society in this way. As a result, they are much more interested in political affairs than they were five years ago.

Batsford tells me that, in the last *Bulletin,* the Society finally got around to setting up a fund for legal fees for libel action and for investigation as a memorial for Newton Armstrong, Jr., the conservative college student in San Diego who, the Birch Society maintains, was murdered by the Communists, although state and local investigators concluded that his hanging was a suicide. Batsford believes that such a fund has been needed for a long time, especially for libel action. His main criticism of Welch was that he goofed by not starting libel action early against the wild charges against the Society.

Our conversation was interrupted at this point by a phone call from some wag, a friend of Batsford, who started by saying, "This is Robert Welch . . ."

Following the call, he continued with the sad observation that there are many people in the Society who don't take it seriously enough to work much. But, he concluded on a hopeful note, the Birch Society can't help but gain strength as long as the problems he mentioned remain. He may be right.

Harold Collins is a pianist who says he gave his first concert at the age of fourteen. He studied under several outstanding teachers and did some further work at Harvard. He now makes a living teaching piano in Gloucester. He is about fifty, single, and lives with his brother in a modest home which boasts a pleasant view of the harbor. Their mother died several years ago and her two sons have kept her room just as she left it. Despite his modest means, Harold Collins managed to scrape together five hundred dollars to purchase a remarkably fine seascape in oils by an artist named Gore.

The name of Harold Collins over the address: 7 Wall Street, Gloucester, Mass., may strike a chord of recollection for a great many readers of "letters to the editor" in newspapers all across the country. For Harold Collins is an inveterate writer of "letters to the editor," and he says he writes to over sixty newspapers.

In the fall of 1961, the Birch Society in Gloucester was involved in a heated election campaign, which revolved around whether or not one of the candidates was a member of the Birch Society. At that time, Harold Collins was the only local member of the Society who chose to acknowledge his membership and he thus emerged as its "spokesman." He helped to define the basic issue of the school-board election as Americanism vs. communism. In conversation he described himself as a long-time conservative and maintained that the Democrats and the Republicans were just two wings on the same rotten bird—that bird, he said, was treason!

In my research on the John Birch Society, I talked with a great many more leaders than regular members. This was partly because leaders were more widely known and more easily indentified. But I also found that a great many ordinary members were rather reluctant to be interviewed. They just didn't understand why I would want to talk with them when I had already talked to local leaders. They were quite content to let the chapter leaders, the co-ordinators, and the Council members speak for them. One other reason for their attitude may be that most of the leaders of the John Birch Society are long-time anti-Communists, while many of the regular members have been only recently introduced to the mysteries of the extreme right wing. But, despite their reluctance to speak for the Society, many of the regular members are full-fledged "true believers." Many of them have written to Robert Welch to express their faith in him and in the Society. Thinking others might be favorably impressed by these letters, Welch has had them included in a pamphlet entitled "Appreciation and Encouragement," which is used for purposes of recruitment.

A housewife in California writes to Welch: "Since the day I saw the film, where you appeared on the screen, I have intended to write you. . . .

"If people who see and hear you on that film are not stirred to their very souls, to want to be a part of this great work you are doing, there must be something wrong. . . ."

A student at Yale writes to Welch: "Again may I thank you for all that you have done and are continuing to do, not only for me, but for this wonderful country of ours—somehow I feel that its destiny lies a great deal in your hands."

A businessman from California writes to a friend in Tennessee saying: "I'm certainly thankful that you introduced us to the John Birch Society. I'm in it with both feet now. I'm leading a chapter; as well as showing *Communism on the Map* and giving an introductory presentation to the Society to groups of people about twice a week. We have had several successful local projects. I think this is really our one last hope."

The mail runs heavy from California and this one is from Arcadia: "May God bless you, Mr. Welch! A very short time ago I was too busy—cleaning house, caring for my family, playing bridge, etc., completely oblivious to what was *really* happening to this wonderful country of ours, and now I'm striving hard to learn all of the things I should have been knowing for the past ten or fifteen years—as a member of the Society. We should get down on our knees to thank God that America has such men as you—and I do!"

Wichita is another center of activity for the Birch Society. A well-indoctrinated member from there writes: "When I first joined The John Birch Society I objected to the words 'traitor' and 'treason' in our booklets, but now I don't believe these words are strong enough to describe the actions of our officials in the State Department, etc. The people must be damned for the rats that they are."

Skaneateles, New York, has a member who is "terribly discouraged, but the activities of The John Birch Society give me one ray of hope."

A parent from Beaumont, Texas says: "Thanks so much for showing us a way in which we may do our best to help. The enclosed five dollars isn't much but I will try to help when I can. Six children require a lot of food and clothes. We are trying to cut expenses every way possible."

Again from California, a member in LaCanada writes: "...since joining the John Birch Society I believe the United States will survive the Communists' threat. Before I couldn't see how in the world we could combat traitors in government, schools, churches, etc. Thank God for John Birch—I'm with you 100% and I'm getting other Americans to join."

A Hoosier writes encouraging Welch to "keep giving it straight—the truth will eventually penetrate, the smears and castigations mean nothing—facts and the truth are the only important items."

An old New Hampshire Yankee writes, saying: "I have clipped out the articles from the Boston *Herald* about you and the work you are doing to bring us back to what I knew fifty to eighty years ago. If the John Birch Society will only continue to work for the two things: fight Communism and work for less government, more responsibility, and a better world, some day we can be saved. With deep respect for a fighting, old fashioned real American...."

Uniting and utilizing the kinds of Council members, organization men, chapter leaders and members that we have seen, Welch has tried to build an organization on two different grounds. The Council members, chapter leaders, and regular members he has bound to the Birch Society with ties of *loyalty* to his "dynamic personal leadership." But the full-time co-ordinators, administrative assistants, and clerical workers have been bound to the Society by bonds of *salary* as well. Even those who feel a deep personal loyalty to Welch—and all of them must at least profess such a loyalty—still have to earn a living. Thus the salaried workers have an "out" when and if they see the Society "sinking." Under such circumstances the "organization men" can "legitimately" abandon the Society on the purely rational grounds that it's no longer functioning properly, quite apart from any "loyalty" to Welch. Despite the efficiency these organization men lend to the Society, the ease with which they can leave is a great weakness for the Society. It is particularly acute because the full-time co-ordinators, who do the organizational leg work, and the office workers, who do the paper work, are all employed on this fairly rational, cut-and-dried, "organization man" basis.

The Birch Society is clearly the most efficiently organized group in the current crop of right-wing organizations. The organization itself is headed by Robert Welch who is "advised" by his Council and, unofficially, by his organization men. The Society has an office staff of salaried administrators and clerical workers numbering about sixty at the home office in Belmont, Massachusetts, plus smaller staffs at the West Coast office in San Marino and at the American Opinion Speakers Bureau in Brookfield, Massachusetts. The Society has a full-time, salaried field staff of about forty co-ordinators. In addition, there are numerous "volunteer" co-ordinators. The local members, numbering between twelve and eighteen thousand, are organized into local chapters of, ideally, from ten to twenty members and are under the direction of a volunteer chapter leader—who is, in turn, under the direction of a co-ordinator. The most important publication of the Society, the monthly *Bulletin,* is geared directly to the local chapter members to provide them with a current interpretation of national and world events and with agenda items for the individual members and for the chapter as a whole.

This, then is the formal hierarchical structure of the Birch Society. It is designed by Welch to utilize what he feels to be the strengths of "dynamic *personal* leadership, around which the split and frustrated and confused forces on our side can be rallied, rapidly and firmly. . . ."[4] In line with this conviction as to the utility and necessity of "charismatic" leadership, Welch insists that the Birch Society is to be a "monolithic body."[5]

CHAPTER VI

Separation of Birch and State

The nation-wide organization of the John Birch Society has equipped it to make a great deal of noise and with considerable effectiveness. One of the major "selling points" used for recruitment is that "the John Birch Society is not just another anti-Communist study group; it is an *action* group." Since its members believe that the Communist conspiracy is active all about them, this emphasis upon *action* has a great deal of appeal.

As the Birch Society swings into action it is directed by an entire set of beliefs, perhaps best described as an ideology, which is very widely and quite consistently held by the members I interviewed. A member might originally have become interested in the Society because of a concern, for example, over the United Nations, the Constitution, income tax, fundamentalist religion, or fluoridation, but as he moves into the Birch Society, he tends to "buy" the entire "line," the entire ideology. The term "ideology" also suggests that economic and political data, in fact all data, are modified by a point of view which may be either rigid or flexible. For instance, if you believe that the sun is the center of our corner of the universe, you "know" that the sun and the moon don't "rise" and "set," but that the earth rotates. Again, if you believe that the Communists control our State Department, you "know" that our country intentionally turned Cuba over to the Russians. The accuracy of the beliefs which make up one's point of view, one's "ideology," determines the accuracy of one's "knowledge." The next two chapters are a statement of the ideological point of view from which members of the Birch Society look upon the world about them, and upon which they act. Many of these ideological beliefs are dead wrong, but you cannot understand or anticipate the thought or the actions of members of the Society without knowing them.

In the ideology of the Birch Society it is contended that an international Communist conspiracy now largely controls not only most of the other nations of the world but also the major social, economic, and political institutions of our own country.[1] The conflict with communism is perceived as the central issue of our time, dominating and overshadowing all others. Unless enough patriots can be aroused in a very short time, "true Americanism" will be completely lost and we will find ourselves enslaved subjects of the Russian Communists. Those in the Society justify their particular ideological beliefs and their activities of social protest in the light of this over-all ideological point of view.

Their acceptance of the belief that Communists are in almost complete control of our country alienates the followers of Welch from their government, from their schools, from their churches, from their neighbors. All are suspect, but especially the Federal Government. Society members want complete separation of their lives from Washington.

Basic for the followers of Welch is a perception of Federal Government as "they" instead of "us." They view Washington almost as the seat of a "foreign" power controlled by those who are indifferent or hostile to the political and economic policies which Birch Society members believe have brought this country to its present greatness. Particularly the older members of the Society with whom I have talked feel that domestic governmental policies have not been acceptable since Hoover, and some, including Welch, would push this dating back to before the administration of Wilson. Welch in the *Blue Book* has a very interesting analysis of what he believes are ten conclusions about government that can be drawn from history.[2] In his first point, Welch clears himself of a charge of anarchy: ". . . government is necessary— some degree of government—in any civilized society." Most of Welch's other points are of little importance because they have not "trickled down" to become a part of the ideology of his followers. But Welch's tenth and concluding point coincides with a non-rational and deep-seated right-wing belief. He says that most of the problems brought on by government would be solved by cutting down its size sharply: ". . . neither the form of government nor its quality is as important as its quantity."

International Policies

Moving on to a consideration of international relations, there seems to be an awareness that isolationism is no longer a viable foreign policy. The Birch Society members I talked with share the belief that we cannot simply ignore the rest of the world, particularly with reference to communism. We must have some sort of relationship to the Communist countries as well as to the other countries in the world. But because the followers of Welch see the leaders and followers of communism as unbelievably strong and unalterably evil, they can entertain no foreign policy that is not dominated by opposition to communism. The fact that there are other economic, political, and social issues unrelated to communism is either unrecognized by them or considered irrelevant. Therefore all foreign policy either "defeats" or "plays into the hands of" the Communists. When the State Department displays a concern for other international problems, it is accused of side-stepping the real issue and of draining our strength. Further, the followers of Welch I met regard as futile any attempt at negotiations with the Russians—even over things, such as disarmament, which are conceivably within the best interests of both countries.

Actions of protest from the Society often accompany such attempted negotiations. For instance, beginning in late July, 1959 an *ad hoc* "front" organization of the Birch Society, the Committee Against Summit Entanglements (C.A.S.E.) , began a drive to stop the proposed exchange of visits between Khrushchev and Eisenhower.[3] C.A.S.E., which did little more than publish full-page newspaper ads, did not prevent their meeting at Camp David or Khrushchev's tour throughout the country. Welch does, however, credit C.A.S.E. and a flood of postcards, letters, and telegrams with helping to dissuade Eisenhower from returning the visit.[4] These appeals warned Eisenhower to "Stay Away U.S.A. The Summit Leads to Disaster!"[5] and advised him: "If you go, don't come back!"[6]

Since the members of the Society I interviewed apparently see no alternatives to an eventual struggle to the death between communism and capitalism (a view shared with most Communists) one would think that they would give military preparation a place of central importance. They do grant such preparation a degree of importance, but (and here they shift ground in their estimate of the actual threat of communism) they believe that if we call their bluff, the Communists will always back down and will retreat rather than fight. Because of this belief, the Society members I interviewed have no real conception or concern regarding the possibility of a nuclear war.

One reason for this apparent disregard of the military may be the fact that a hard-line, pro-military ideological position would be fully as suicidal for the Society in the current American scene as would an aggressive anti-Semitism. For with a pro-military ideological stance to add substance to their charge, those antagonistic to the Society would have ample justification for labeling the Birch Society "Fascist."

But despite the fact that the Society has no ideological belief regarding the military, some of the Society's strongest and most active protests have been in behalf of strongly anti-Communist military figures, both active and retired.

One of the most dramatic had to do with the support of a well-known figure of the far right, Major General Edwin Walker, in his radically right-wing efforts to indoctrinate the troops under his command in Germany. For this activity Walker was investigated, relieved of his command, and admonished by the Secretary of the Army. Citing the case of General Walker, along with many other instances of the participation of military personnel in the "alerting" of the public as well as the troops through public "cold-war seminars," Senator Fulbright, in a memorandum to Secretary of Defense McNamara, made public in June of 1961, "questioned the right of military officers to make statements critical of the nation's domestic and foreign policies."[7] This whole problem of military participation in public affairs, a reversal of the historic position of the military in this country, came to the fore as a result of a National Security directive of 1958, indicating that the military was to assume a role in the indoctrination, not only of troops, but of the public as well in the face of the menace and tactics of communism. Fulbright suggested the revision of this directive on the basis of the fact that military officers do not have the background or experience to make them balanced authorities on non-military matters. Evidence cited by him for this conclusion was, in addition to the case of Walker, the use in these militarily sponsored cold-war seminars of "extremely radical right-wing" materials and speakers, who emphasized the "theme that the primary, if not exclusive, danger to this country is internal Communist infiltration. Past and current international difficulties are often attributed to this or ascribed to 'softness,' 'sellouts,' 'appeasements,' etc." In addition to these points of view on international affairs, Fulbright also noted that these materials and speakers often equated "social legislation with socialism and socialism with communism." Therefore, "much of the Administration's domestic legislative program, including continuation of the graduated income tax, expansion of Social Security (particularly medical care under Social Security), federal aid to education, etc., under this philosophy would be characterized as steps toward communism."[8]

Fulbright said that military persons should be allowed to continue attendance at and participation in public occasions devoted to consideration of unclassified military matters. But he suggested that they should be restrained in their sponsorship, attendance, and participation in non-military public occasions. The Defense Department concurred and with this the conflict "escalated." The charge was made by Senator Thurmond that Fulbright had "muzzled the military." Thurmond called for an investigation of Defense Department censorship of the speeches of officers and of the admonishment of Major General Walker. This investigation drew the full support of the Birch Society. Welch urged his followers to *"Support Senator Thurmond's demand for the investigation of the military gag rule. This is the* most IMPORTANT *item in this month's agenda."*[9] Welch went on for the next five pages describing the situation, its significance, and urging that letters be written to all the Senators he had listed as involved in the proposed hearing. A parallel and more local campaign was begun in Arkansas and participated in by members of the Birch Society to contest Fulbright's Senate seat in the Arkansas Democratic primary in the summer of 1962. Possible contenders were Governor Faubus or Representative Alford, and the central issue was to be Fulbright's "muzzling of the military." This campaign aborted. Apparently Fulbright's position was too secure for either Faubus or Alford to challenge him successfully.

The hearings proposed by Thurmond and supported by the Birch Society began in September, 1961. But neither the anticipated exoneration of Walker, nor the "exposure" of some sort of vast web of internal subversion ever materialized.

It would seem that the most important role of military leadership, according to the Birch Society, is to join them in alerting and awakening the American people! Apparently our military leaders are to warn Americans about the civilian leaders under whom they serve. It would seem quite in line with a logical extension of this kind of reasoning—if at some time these military leaders plotted *Seven Days In May*.

National Sovereignty

The Birch Society members I talked with see this country, once it is purged of "internal subversion," as the strongest bulwark against the advance of communism. This view, united with a wistful lingering isolationism, dictates for the followers of Welch the imperative of maintaining and enhancing our national sovereignty. Surely *uninterrupted* enhancement of our national power and prestige is an unrealistic goal in a world where numerous nations are in a position to defend and pursue their own interests. But other nations are viewed by members of the Society only in terms of whether they're on "our side" in this "central" conflict with communism. This is the only criterion other nations have to meet to earn the Birchers' approval.

Any governments—even dictatorships—as long as they claim to be staunchly anti-Communist, are supported by Welch and his followers. This was the basis of Welch's support for Batista and the main reason that he attacked Castro as "a Communist" as soon as he became a major threat to the regime of Batista. The avowed anticommunism of Trujillo, the late dictator of the Dominican Republic, was also the reason his country had such a low percentage of Communist infiltration in the "Scoreboard" issue of *American Opinion* for the summer of 1960. It was then seen as only 10 to 30 per cent under Communist influence. Even lower ratings were given to Salazar's Portugal, and to Franco's Spain.

The willingness of the Society to support anti-Communist leaders was further illustrated by the active support of Tshombe in the Congo. Tshombe had only to give assurances that his secessionist Katanga was anti-Communist, and several Birch Society leaders joined the "American Committee for aid to Katanga Freedom Fighters." This organization provided these Birch Society leaders with the welcome opportunity to support an anti-Communist government and to attack the United Nations at the same time. The "American Committee for Aid to Katanga Freedom Fighters" placed two full-page ads in the New York *Times* and many other papers at the height of the Congo crisis. The first ad, appearing December 14, 1961, proclaimed: "Katanga is the Hungary of 1961!" Among the eighty listed signers were at least nine men at the time active in leadership of the Birch Society. A second ad appeared January 12, 1962, in which this committee asked rhetorically, "On the Evidence from Katanga: Shall We Bail the UN Out of Bankruptcy?" Following the first ad, the nine leaders from the Birch Society had been publicly identified; this time only one of them was listed among the partial list of signers.

Neutralist Nations

As we have seen, anti-Communist governments, even dictatorships, are enthusiastically supported by the Society. But neutralist nations are quite another thing. The neutralist policy of nonalignment is both unacceptable and suspect as far as Welch and his followers are concerned. Neutral nations are therefore regarded by the Society as cowards or, more likely, as covert collaborators with the Communists. On the same grounds, extremist Communists may, of course, regard the neutralists as "covert collaborators with the capitalists."

The United Nations

In line with their emphasis upon national sovereignty, our participation in the UN is grudgingly accepted only at the level of a public forum. The Birch Society members I interviewed were almost unanimous in a very strong antipathy toward the UN. The prospect of granting authority over any aspects of our international relationship to a governmental body other than our own is, for the Birch Society out of the question.

The Birch Society has always carried criticism of the UN and its various agencies in its *Bulletins.* Halloween and Christmas have always been seasons when the Society has turned its wrath upon the United Nations Children's Fund (UNICEF), protesting in turn the Halloween collection by children of UNICEF funds to feed starving children and the sale of UNICEF Christmas Cards for the same purpose. The Society has given wide distribution to a reprint entitled, "Don't Send Me a UNICEF Greeting Card" and for the last two years has printed Christmas cards of its own—but there seems to be no indication that the proceeds from *these* cards, at two dollars per dozen, are used to feed little children. The amount is said to cover only the cost of printing and mailing.

Up until the beginning of 1962, the attacks upon the UN by the Birch Society were random in nature. But starting in January of that year, a regular item on the agenda of the monthly *Bulletins* was a drive to "Get the U.S. out of the U.N." Welch inaugurated this sustained attack with the statement that "the time has clearly come to recognize the Fifth Communist Internationale for what it really is; and to do all we can to break its closing grip on our freedom and our independence."[10]

There are a number of charges that members of the Society make about the UN. The American Association for the United Nations, 345 East 46 Street, New York 17, New York,[11] has found these misrepresentations so persistent that it has been necessary to devote considerable effort to countering them with factual information. The charges that I have heard most frequently from members of the Society are rebutted in the following statements from the AAUN.

The charge: The United Nations is atheistic because God is not named in the UN Charter. The facts:

The UN General Assembly opens and closes its sessions with a moment of silence for prayer or meditation.

The Meditation Room at UN Headquarters is open to delegates and secretariat members for meditation or prayer.

The Constitution of the United States does not name God. Certainly this does not make this document, or our nation upon which it is based, ungodly.

The charge: The United Nations is too costly. The United States pays all the bills. The facts:

The regular budget of the UN for 1962 is $82 million. The United States pays 32.02 percent of this budget. In addition, there are voluntary contributions to special and extraordinary expenses such as Technical Assistance, Congo operation, Refugees, etc. The cost to each United States citizen, therefore, is $1.06.

The annual cost to the United States of its United Nations Contributions is about equal to what 10 hours of World War II cost our nation.

The charge: The Soviet Union dominates the United Nations. The facts:

At the same time that we hear this accusation, the Soviet Union spreads the propaganda that it is the United States which controls the UN.

There are one hundred and four member nations in the United Nations. Of this number, ten states are under Soviet domination and an additional one, Yugoslavia, which has broken with the Soviet Union, frequently votes with that nation.

Thus, there are 94 nations that are not satellites of the Soviet Union. Such member nations as the Latin American countries, the United Kingdom and the Western European states are friendly to the United States. The member nations from Africa and Asia will, like those named above, vote according to the merits of the question, and according to their own national interests.

The charge: The UN Charter was written by Alger Hiss. The facts:

No one individual nor delegate from any one nation was the architect of the United Nations. During World War II, there were committees in various countries meeting to study what international organization would take the place of the League of Nations.

As for the United States, the Secretary of State (Cordell Hull) set up a series of planning committees, one of which was to draft the constitution for the organization later to be known as the United Nations. The first United States working draft of the UN Charter was written by: Isaiah Bowman, President of Johns Hopkins University; James T. Shotwell, distinguished Columbia University historian; Hamilton Fish Armstrong, Editor of Foreign Affairs quarterly; Benjamin V. Cohen, Counsel of the Department of State; and Clark M. Eichelberger, Director of the League of Nations Association. The committee met under the Chairmanship of State Sumner Welles. (Designation and titles are given as of the time of the Committee.)

Alger Hiss had nothing to do with this original draft. He was at Dumbarton Oaks where a later draft was prepared for the San Francisco Conference. At San Francisco, he was given an executive post called Secretary-General of the Conference and, as such, was removed from a policy forming post with the United States Delegation. The job of Secretary-General of a conference is a mechanical one.

The United States Delegation to the San Francisco Conference was composed of: Senators Arthur Vandenberg and Tom Connally; Representatives Sol Bloom and Charles Eaton; Commander Harold Stassen; Miss Virginia Gildersleeve, President of Barnard College; with Secretary of State Edward R. Stettinius, Jr., as Chairman. Former Secretary of State Cordell Hull served as Senior Advisor. (Titles are given as of 1945.) The present U.S. Ambassador to the UN, Adlai E. Stevenson, served as an advisor to the Delegation.

Forty-two national organizations were asked by our government to send consultants to the Conference. Such organizations as the American Legion, Veterans of Foreign Wars, U.S. Chamber of Commerce, National Association of Manufacturers, American Federation of Labor and Congress of Industrial Organizations were so represented.

The charge: A Soviet General is the Permanent Chairman of the UN Military Staff Committee. The facts:

Article 47 of the UN Charter states that "there shall be established a Military Staff Committee to advise and assist the Security Council on all questions relating to the Security Council's military requirements for the maintenance of international peace and security, the employment and command of forces placed at its disposal, the regulation of armaments, and possible disarmament."

Because of disagreement among the great powers which compose the Committee, the Military Staff Committee has never functioned and therefore, it has had nothing to do with UN police forces. Chairmanship of the Committee has always been on a rotating basis.

I am under no illusions that "statements of fact" from any source besides the home office of the Birch Society in Belmont will influence the hard-core membership of the Society, but others of us welcome a little more variety in our sources of information.

Internal Subversion

Members of the Birch Society believe that our national sovereignty is being threatened from many quarters. They see the "erosion" of national sovereignty in the inclusion of our NATO allies in formulation of our foreign policy and in our continuing and deepening of responsible relationships with the UN. But this "erosion" proceeds apace even at home, according to the followers of Welch. As a matter of fact, the Birch Society estimated that the United States was, even in 1960, 40 per cent to 60 per cent under Communist control.

This is a *minimum* estimate. We believe there is in the American people a great latent strength not yet rotted by all of the infiltration, indoctrination, and political sabotage to which we have been subjected. And we believe Americans are at last beginning to realize that their very lives are at stake.

But actual Communist control at the present time is terribly obvious. Of the four presidential and vice-presidential candidates, two [Kennedy and Lodge] have openly served Communist purposes in the Senate and the "United Nations" respectively. The other two [Nixon and Johnson] are admired as shrewd opportunists. But indications are that the campaigns will be conducted in terms of platitudes, evasions, and open bribery of votes—with never a realistic mention of the International Communist Conspiracy that now threatens the life of every decent American. There are two possible explanations: either (a) the conspirators controlled the nomination of the candidates, or (b) the conspiracy is so powerful that the candidates dare not offend it by recognizing its existence. Take your choice.[12]

We have long had more or less concealed Communists in almost all branches of our Federal Government. Now we visibly have more of them, and they are less concealed. And now we have Communist influence, easily recognizable by all serious students of the conspiracy, exercising high degrees of control in many of our state governments as well.

Members of Congress have openly urged abolition of the Committee on Un-American Activities because its slight powers vex traitors. In San Francisco a gang of degenerates, bred in our colleges [sic], attacked the Committee in one of the "student riots" the Communist conspiracy staged throughout the world, and no one dared to demand revocation of the federal scholarships held by many of these disgusting creatures. Senator Kennedy, by pressing for repeal of the student loyalty oath, in effect claimed that it is the duty of American taxpayers to pay for the education of their future murderers.

Never before has treason been so brazen and so audacious. Our State Department, which created Soviet Cuba, is now using the power of the United States to make another Cuba of the Dominican Republic. We have suspended testing of nuclear weapons for only one conceivable purpose—to give the Soviet time to attain, or at least claim, superiority in weapons of which propaganda has engendered in us an hysterical fear. No one dares to say that *all* available evidence indicates that the pilot of our famous U-2 must have purposely landed his plane in Russia; and that objectives of those who planned the incident must have been: (1) to give the Soviet a model to duplicate; (2) to provide the American Communists with an excuse for getting reconnaissance over Russia suspended; and (3) to postpone the "Summit Conference" with a maximum of public disgrace to the United States.

These are but a few of the thousand indications of a control the Communists veil only by the most transparent pretexts. But even half a million *really dedicated* Americans, organized for effective action, could yet utterly destroy the obscene incubus that is paralyzing our nation.[13]

The members of the Society see not only overt "subversion," described fantastically as in the above, but "subversion" in more covert forms as well. There are two main types of this "covert" subversion which may be described (1) as an "undercutting of initiative and incentive," and (2) as a "drive toward totalitarianism."

The "undercutting of incentive and initiative" is seen as taking place in the two major areas of taxation and social-welfare programs.

Taxation

Progressive taxation, especially, is held up as stifling initiative. There is a great deal of complaint, particularly about a 92 per cent tax rate on yearly incomes of one million or over, a problem not faced by most of us.

Not only do the Birch Society members perceive the progressive income tax as a "covert" move toward communism, but they also see rises in the general rates of taxation in local and state governments as a move in the same direction.

Welfare

Social-welfare programs are also viewed by the followers of Welch as "steps toward the point at which our nation can be comfortably merged with international Communism." They so view social security, medical care for the aging, workmen's compensation, unemployment compensation, and other local, state, and federal governmental welfare programs. Within a larger frame of reference, they perceive governmentally provided "security" as the "bait" for the "hook" of "totalitarianism." There is also a fairly strong anti-intellectual streak of distrust of the "egg heads" who, they feel, conceive these social-welfare programs. Many members of the Society feel that all of these programs, as well as taxation, undercut the "incentive" and "initiative" of the American people.

Speaking directly to this point of view, many observers are justifiably disturbed over the casual granting to the Birch Society and other right-wing groups the title of "anti-Communists." They are not, these observers feel, "anti-Communists" in any sense. They are fighting not over communism, but over the domestic political and economic issues of progressive income tax, the union shop, social security, workmen's compensation, unemployment benefits, and other welfare programs, and ought not to be dignified with the title of "anti-Communists." I would concur in this, but would grant to most members of the Birch Society the "sincerity" of their belief that they are actually fighting communism.

The Supreme Court

The members of the Birch Society believe any "attack upon individual initiative" to be a part of some sort of "drive toward totalitarianism." They see this "totalitarian drive" as a "conspiracy" between the Supreme Court and the President against Congress. To help put this view in some perspective, we should remember that since Eisenhower proved a disappointment or even since the Supreme Court "began reading the election returns" during Roosevelt's first term, the American right wing has felt it had "trustworthy" friends only in Congress.

The Birch Society centers its hostility against this "subversive perversion of the Constitution" by the Supreme Court upon Chief Justice Earl Warren. The Society and its members have a long list of "grievances" which "prove" that Warren is nothing but an agent for the Communists. First of all, he keeps handing down decisions that say that the Bill of Rights applies to American Communists. Now nearly any member of the Birch Society could tell you right off that Communist Party members shouldn't have any legal rights—and he could name others that shouldn't either. Certainly the list would include Communist sympathizers, and, after all, unwitting Communist dupes are the most dangerous of all. Thinking for only a moment, he could name a long list of Communist dupes: labor leaders, "modernist" ministers, nearly all college professors, the "unwitting" agents of the CIA, all of TVA, those in the mass media, PTA's, the United States Chamber of Commerce, the NAM, and, as the words of the song by the Chad Mitchell Trio go, "There's no one left but me and thee—and we're not sure of thee!" But, I digress—of course Warren and his cohorts in the Court are wrong in applying the Bill of Rights to all our citizens. But the members of the Society have a great many other commendable reasons why Warren should be watched. He "stirred up dissension" with the School Desegregation Decision of 1954—a typical Communist trick! He disregards "States Rights." What's he trying to do—force the States into some sort of a federation? What's more, Warren's Court has failed to issue injunctions to stop Eisenhower, Kennedy, or Johnson from doing any number of things at home and abroad of which the Birch Society

and its right-wing idols in Congress disapprove. But worst of all—
and here's where the average member of the Birch Society, who's
actually sat down and read through the Constitution, really has
the poor old Chief Justice of the United States—as any fool can see,
Warren "disregards" the "original intentions" of our founding
fathers. That clinches it. And that's why the Birch Society gives
top priority to "The Movement To Impeach Earl Warren."

The "drive" to impeach Warren has been given added im-
petus since the assassination of President Kennedy. In the *Bulletin*
for January, 1964, Welch added three more reasons for his impeachment:

(1) He took the lead, immediately behind Khrushchev himself, in blaming the crime on the anti-Communists, even though he did not have a
scintilla of evidence to justify the accusation, and it soon proved to be
exactly contrary to the facts. This utterly unjudicial and inflammatory action on the part of the highest judge in our nation has shocked a lot of
people besides ourselves.

(2) Even after it became clear that the assassin was a self-proclaimed
Marxist with a long record of Communist activities and affiliations, Warren has brazenly continued to proclaim the exact Khrushchev line,
blaming the Communist crime on the very people who have done the
most to expose and prevent the appproaching Communist reign of terror
in our country. In this connection and on this subject, there has been practically no distinction between the statements issued by Warren and the
lies published by the Communist press.

(3) Regardless of the other effects and significances of the above actions,
they should certainly cause any self-respecting judge to disqualify himself
from serving on any judicial body to investigate the very crime which he
so hastily prejudged, and on which he has expressed such a strong bias
in favor of those who appear to be most directly involved as planners,
participants, or accomplices. Instead Warren has brazenly accepted appointment for the very commission set up to pre-empt all investigation
of the murder and the forces behind it.

Petitions with space for fifty names are included in the
"Warren Impeachment Packet" and additional copies are available from the Society at $1.00 for 20, $3.00 for 100, or $20.00 for

1,000. As soon as each petition is filled with fifty names it is to be returned to "The Movement To Impeach Earl Warren," Belmont 78, Massachusetts—the home office. To date the only thing that has been done has been to "tabulate" and store them. The next move seems to be up to Robert Welch. Whether he will forward these petitions to the House of Representatives, announce the total number of signatures, publish the names of all the signers, or paper the walls of the home office with them is still very much up in the air—but the drive to collect them still proceeds apace. The faithful members of the Society spend a great deal of time signing one another's petitions. They also put up signs along the highway and occasionally take to the streets with placards.

Who knows what might inspire another Oswald? Of course it's possible that the next psychopathic assassin might be a left-winger, too—but the odds are against it.

On Wednesday, February 13, 1963, a young man from Phoenix, Arizona drove his car up onto the steps of the Department of Justice, crawled underneath it and told surprised and somewhat bemused Justice Department building guards that he would set off a bomb wired to the bottom of the car unless he were allowed to talk to FBI Director J. Edgar Hoover about "the impeachment of Warren, the impeachment of the President and his entire Cabinet, and about rackets in the U.S. Government." He confidently informed the guards that "J. Edgar Hoover knows what I'm here for." After finally flushing the man out from under his car with tear gas, the police and army personnel, who had also become involved in the episode, were relieved to find that the suitcase "bomb" contained nothing but newspapers and a flashlight. The man had been under psychiatric care but had passed a sanity hearing some three weeks earlier.[14] There was no indication in the newspaper report that this apparently disturbed man was a member of the Birch Society. And there is no reason that he would have to be a member to be acquainted with the "movement" to impeach Warren which has been fairly widely publicized and which has had fairly strong support (especially in the Southeast) by the rest of the American right wing.

In the June, 1963, issue of *American Opinion,* Westbrook Pegler used his entire column to lament the fact that the would-be assassin who tried to shoot President-elect Franklin D. Roosevelt in February, 1933, missed and killed Mayor Cermak of Chicago instead. Pegler admits that "public opinion might say it would serve me right to be drawn and quartered for this evil speculation." But there can be a wide gap between the reaction of public opinion and that of a hate-driven psychopath.

There have been other incidents of intemperate and violent acts. In California, the home of a minister who was an outspoken opponent of local right-wing extremists, was bombed, as was the local office of the American Association for the United Nations. The Birchers said it must have been the Communists. There are often rashes of obscene and threatening phone calls directed against other liberal spokesmen. Welch has dismissed the charge that members of the Birch Society are involved in such things because they were "responsible citizens who simply did not engage in such childish and futile nonsense as anonymous phone calls." But, interestingly enough, Welch added to this assertion a pleading and a warning to his followers. "Let's keep this assurance completely justified under any and all provocations.[15] The anonymous letters received by public opponents of the Birch Society such as California's Senator Kuchel reek with hate and libel. Anonymous letters, phone calls and certainly bombings would never be sanctioned by Welch or by the home office of the Birch Society. And Welch is so convinced that he addresses only the mentally stable when he speaks to his followers that he simply cannot conceive of them doing any of these things. But the tragically illustrated fact remains that inflammatory charges such as the ones Welch and his followers have made about Warren, Kennedy, Stevenson, Eisenhower, Nixon, the ADA, the NAACP, the ACLU, the NCC (to name but a few) can, to the mentally unstable, serve as an incitement to violence—even though the inflammatory language was never intended to inflame but only to "shock" and to "alert" the "apathetic."

Welch and his followers feel themselves driven to "shock" and to "alert" the American people. They are driven by the conviction that our national leaders in government are, intentionally or not, capitulating piecemeal to the Communists.

CHAPTER VII

Its Shape Upon the Land

The Birch Society attack upon our government centers upon Washington. But when one speaks of their attacks upon schools, churches, labor unions, newspapers and the like, one is describing Birch Society conflict at the local level.

Education

Education is, of course, a prime target for any group seeking to propagate a particular ideology. And the members of the Society believe not only that the leaders of our Federal Government are leading us toward "a Communist takeover" but also that our schools are similarly corrupting the youth and children of our country.

When the members of the Society think about education, they think of "brainwashing"—and they are considered one and the same. Education is seen in no sense as the development of critical capacities of thought, as the development within the individual of the capacity to discover, use, and re-evaluate his own criteria of truth, beauty, and goodness. Brainwashing alone is held to be the basic process of education at all levels including those of higher education. Welch speaks of the institutions of higher "leaning" in Boston. And primary and secondary education, his followers believe, has been in the hands either of liberals or incompetents, who have failed to teach the "real fundamentals." Thus the task for members of the Birch Society is two-pronged.

The "Real Fundamentals"

First they must make sure that the "real fundamentals" are taught, especially in grade school. The emphasis on the "real fundamentals," of course, antedates John Dewey and his experience-centered and interest-centered curriculum. The "Three R's" are to be primary, and education is to concentrate on reading, handwriting, arithmetic, English, and "patriotic history." Reading is to be taught through the use of phonics and the largest possible vocabulary is to be inculcated. In line with this there has actually been republication of the *McGuffey Readers*.

Debate has always raged over what teaching methods are best and what content is proper for presentation to children and youth. Similar debate, particularly upon teaching methods has raged within professional educational circles through the centuries. Members of the Birch Society would contend for a limited curriculum with ideologically acceptable content and for traditional teaching methods. As they find most public educational institutions unacceptable at these points, efforts of local Birch Society members are concentrated upon urging the return to an "original purity," to an idealized distant past, through pressure on school boards and administrators or, if these efforts fail, upon support or establishment of "acceptable" private schools.

Gloucester, Massachusetts, has been one of many communities that has had to contend with this kind of purge, promoted by its chapter of the Birch Society. This seaport town witnessed a knockdown, drag-out fight when members of the Society waged a successful campaign to get their candidate elected to the school board. The Birchers were able to get the campaign defined as a conflict between "Americanism and communism" and they were also able to sell their candidate as a "champion of the people" battling against "the intellectuals" and "the behind-the-scenes power structure." "The people," thus led, rose up and elected the Birch-backed candidate.

Counter-Brainwashing

While those adjudged "incompetent" because they refuse to limit themselves to the "real fundamentals" are being dealt with by local members of the Society, "liberal" influence must be erased by "counter-brainwashing." This is most effectively done in adult study groups such as local chapters of the Birch Society in which

the "self-evident truths" of anti-Communist authors and leaders
are presented for admiration, further illustration, and acceptance
—but seldom or never for critical evaluation. But there have been
occasional efforts by members of the Society to provide such
"study groups" for junior-high and high-school students. In one
town a leader runs a Saturday morning "class" in American History and there are other such "classes" offered in California and
other centers of Birch Society strength.

Not only must there be counter-brainwashing to mitigate
the past influence of liberals, there must also be efforts to stamp
out any continuing liberal influence of teachers, administrators,
or texts.

One of the directives from Welch urges members to infiltrate their PTA's and to make these groups into a nucleus for the
Birch Society ideology of education. But the main Society protest
activity has come, not through infiltration of PTA's, but in attacks
upon individual teachers—especially high-school social-studies
teachers (a student's bringing a concealed tape recorder into the
classroom in Paradise, California was one example), and upon
what the Society believes to be objectionable textbooks. The usual
pattern has been to raise questions about textbooks at any of a
number of major or minute points of authorship, references cited,
or content. Finding objectionable sources or content, members of
the Society propose either more "Americanist" or more advanced
tests. Sometimes these come in a package deal such as the "Planned
Patriotism Program" promoted by right-wing groups in the Phoenix
area. Such proposals are nearly sure to create conflict within a
community, and, with the issue already defined by the local Birch
Society as "communism *vs* Americanism," the character of the conflict is inevitably acrimonious. The issues move rather naturally
into the political contests for school boards and into proposals for
such things as the decentralization of school districts and for
"local option" on textbooks, so Birch Society members and
other right-wingers may exercise more control in the local schools.

The Contagion of Ideas

Ideas themselves are regarded by Birch Society members almost as "germs," and bad ones must be stamped out lest they pro-

duce "mental infection." Therefore anybody who has been exposed to these "germs" at Harvard (or nearly any American college or university—because, as one Society member pointed out,
there are only three "safe" colleges in the United States), at the
London School of Economics (where the late President Kennedy
studied when his father was the Ambassador to England), or as a
Rhodes Scholar, is immediately suspect as a "carrier" of these
"germs." On the same basis, a textbook is suspect if its author,
or any other author referred to in footnotes or suggested bibli-
ography, is such a "carrier."

It is interesting to note that no equally infectious power is
attributed by Birch Society members to their own brand of
"Americanist" ideas. One can only infer from this attitude that
the "Americanist" ideas of the Birch Society can be accepted by
a student only if there is no competition against them. The defensive stance against "unsafe" or "harmful" ideas is very similar
to "pure from the world" sectarian religious thought.

Since Birch Society members do not see the educational process as developing critical capacities of thought within the individual, the followers of Welch have no concept of a market place in
which a student is taught to evaluate ideas. The market place is
far too dangerous—come over here and just listen to Welch,
they would counsel. This is certainly a major contradiction to
their proclamation of the integrity of the individual.

Religion

Members of the Society believe that religious leaders as well
as schoolteachers ought to uphold, teach, and preach what the
Birch Society defines as the "fundamental truths." But as they
look about them in their local communities, the followers of
Welch "spot" many religious leaders who, they feel, have abandoned these "fundamental truths." How are they to deal with
these "renegades"? In the fields of government and education we
have seen how members of the Society despise and, whenever
possible, attack all but their ideological allies. The same is true
in religion with one major exception—most of the people in this
country will not "buy" a group which openly attacks the minority

religious groupings of Roman Catholics and Jews. But it seems that it is acceptable to attack and to vilify the Protestant denominations—perhaps because they are not painted as an "underdog" due to their historical position of middle- and upper-class power and influence.

It is notable that many among the Birch Society leaders and regular members I interviewed had no active religious affiliation—and none had more than nominal affiliation. Their membership in the Birch Society was by far their most time- and interest-consuming voluntary association. The John Birch Society has become their church, accepted as God's vessel of salvation, as God present with them for guidance, for comfort, and for strength. Welch has become the revealer of God's eternal truths, their John the Baptist who will lay his hand upon the Savior yet to come. So overshadowing has become the fear of communism that some in our midst thus seek salvation. A member of the Birch Society could rightly argue that none of this terminology is explicit —that no member would describe the Birch Society as his "church," nor would any describe Welch as their religious leader. But from a background of study in the sociology of religion as well as preparation for and service in the Christian ministry, I feel justified in identifying, and protesting, the fact that the Birch Society and its leader serve both as functional alternatives to the Church and to its Lord.[1] Religion, in short, has come to be something that they use for their *own* purpose rather than a relationship to a God who uses them for *His* purposes. Many Birch Society members will probably not even understand this distinction.

How then, do they relate themselves to the major religious grouping of this country? Religious institutions and beliefs are of importance to the Birch Society members I interviewed only as propagandistic and psychological supports for the economic and political ideological beliefs they hold as central. Religious beliefs become of secondary importance and are perceived as "not worth fighting over." Welch and the Birch Society members interviewed are willing to "forget" their religious differences and to concentrate their attention upon the "really important" tasks at hand. Having found a spiritual home in the Birch Society, members turn to the major religious groupings nationally and locally only to search for anti-Communist allies and to ferret out those who appear to be subversives.

The Birch Society has found some ideological allies among the Roman Catholic hierarchy and among Protestant sectarian-fundamentalists. Roman Catholics from the conservative wing of the Church tend to be attracted to the anti-Communist position of the Birch Society, though they endorse it at a rather naïve level. For instance, the early and benevolent endorsement by Cardinal Cushing of Welch and the Birch Society, so widely publicized by the Society, has proved to be an embarrassment to him and he has since taken pains to describe the Society as "a good thing gone wrong."

The sectarian fundamentalist followers of such religious leaders as Carl McIntire, and Billy James Hargis are attracted not only to the Birch Society's anticommunism, but also to its conservative economic and political views.

Denominational Protestantism with its educated ministry and administrative leadership has long since moved theologically beyond Biblical literalism—the basis of many so-called fundamental doctrines for the Protestant sectarian-fundamentalists—into a deeper grappling with issues of Biblical criticism and theological doctrines. Denominational Protestants are far from united in the Biblical interpretations and doctrinal positions to which they have come, but the simplistic answers of the fundamentalists are unacceptable to nearly all of them.

Within Denominational Protestantism there is also a reluctance to accept a simplistic identification of conservative "Americanism" or economics with the Christian Gospel—an identification represented, for instance, in the publications *The Cross and Flag* and *Christian Economics*. The similar reluctance of some Protestants of an existentialist or neo-orthodox position is based upon the unpredictability of the movement of God in the lives of men and in history—and a consequent reluctance to presume to anticipate God's leading. With other Protestants, of a liberal theological position in the social gospel, the disinclination to make such identification rests upon a belief that God's judgment falls upon America as well as upon other nations. Economic and political affairs, therefore, ought to follow not "laws" of their own but the will of God, and therefore ought to provide basic necessities, equal economic opportunities, and equal political expression to God's children all over the world, regardless of race or nationality.

National Council of Churches

A great deal of criticism, often shading into vilification, has been directed toward the major Protestant denominations as they are united in the National Council of Churches, which offers an attractive target to the Birch Society for two reasons. First, as in governmental and educational fields, much of the leadership of the National Council has been accused by right-wingers of open, hidden, or witless co-operation with Communist goals and agents. These accusations are based largely upon their alleged affiliation or co-operation with allegedly Communist or "Communist infiltrated" organizations or "fronts." The so-called Circuit Riders have been expecially industrious in the compilation of these "citations." For a careful and thorough study of the validity of charges of this type, see Philip Wogaman's *The Methodist-Ministry and Communism—The Truth Behind the Charges.*[2]

Secondly, liberal Protestants have, of course, been able at times to express liberal economic and political views through statements released by the National Council upon various issues. These statements are explicitly presented as speaking "to" rather than "for" its member churches. Nevertheless, the Birch Society has seized upon the statements and the accusations against Council leaders in an attempt to label the National Council of Churches as "pro-Communist" and to get less liberal leaders, local churches, and denominations to withdraw from it—thereby trying to rob of any possible religious sanction economic and political views with which they disagree. An example of such an attack is *A Report to the Vestry of St. Mark's Episcopal Church, Shreveport, Louisiana, on the National Council of the Churches of Christ in the United States of America.*[3] This booklet has been widely circulated within the right wing. Particularly bothersome issues for the committee which rendered this report seemed to be those statements of the National Council regarding federal aid to education, the so-called right-to-work laws, the ethical considerations of the 1962 steel dispute, the seating of Communist China in the United Nations, and the Christian view of Negro integration.

To further buttress these attacks upon the National Council of Churches, and upon the major Protestant denominations, Birch Society members strike at their religious teachings, comparing them unfavorably with those of the sectarian "fundamentalists" who alone are given credit for knowing and speaking the "fundamental truths." This affinity of Birch Society members and others of the right wing for religious-economic-political "fundamentalism" has helped to account for the construction of a number of plush, modern sectarian-fundamentalist churches in Texas and Southern California. And I, myself, was told by a number of Birch Society members that a young Methodist minister with the "right" religious views, "could go a long way."

The "Subversive" Christian Clergy

Robert Welch, whose religious affiliation, if any, is never mentioned, has a deep distrust of the Christian clergy. In the *Blue Book,* Welch bemoans the shrinking number of truly dedicated religious fundamentalists.

... fully one-third of the services in at least the Protestant churches of America are helping that trend. For the ministers themselves are *not* true believers in the Divine Names or the Divine History and Divine Teachings to which they give lip service, as they go through their conventional motions on Sunday mornings. Some have merely watered down the faith of our fathers, and of theirs, into an innocuous philosophy instead of an evangelistic religion. Some have converted Christianity into a so-called "social gospel," that bypasses all questions of dogma with an indifference which is comfortable to both themselves and their parishioners; and which "social gospel" becomes in fact indistinguishable from advocacy of the welfare state by socialist politicians. And some actually use their pulpits to preach outright Communism, often in very thin disguise if any, while having the hypocrisy as atheists to thank God in public for their progressive apostacy.[4]

Such a statement is quite a surprise coming from one who is not a religious leader and who lays no claim to regular Sunday worship. Welch, however, presumes to speak not only for all of Protestantism, but for all the religions of the world. He says "it may shock the Protestants among you to have these things said out loud, but you know in your hearts that they are true. It is also true that while later, perhaps slower, and not yet so far advanced in some cases, the same trend of world disillusionment and loss of true faith is visible among Catholics, among Jews, among Moslems, among Buddhists, and among the formerly devout believers of every great religion of the world."[5] As I said, it is somewhat surprising to see Welch emerge as such an outstanding religious authority. But perhaps this is fitting, for his followers do, indeed, regard him as some sort of "savior."

In his public addresses since founding the Birch Society, Welch has often returned to this theme of "subversion" in the Protestant ministry. Speaking in Dallas, Texas, more than two years before that city became the scene of the tragic assassination of President Kennedy, Welch repeated his standard string of charges.[6] He told an audience of 1,400 Texans that Americans may be living in a Communist-controlled slave state "in just a few years." He told his responsive audience that this probably would result from internal forces of subversion and "treason in our government" and not from an outside military force. He continued to jab at Protestant ministers, saying that only about 3 per cent of those in the United States are Communists, but that they have maneuvered themselves into powerful positions. He suggested that "no blame can be attached to the other ninety-seven per cent except for the same gullibility with which Americans as a whole are afflicted."

In response to charges like these, Rev. William H. Dickinson, pastor of Dallas' Highland Park Methodist Church told his congregation: "Accusing another person of disloyalty to the nation or to the Christian faith is serious business and can lead to great danger. But far more deceitful and far more perilous than to call a man or insinuate that a man is a Communist when he is not is to call yourself a Christian when you are not."

Welch continued his speaking tour into California where he

repeated his charge against the Protestant clergy. But there he encountered another outspoken leader of the Methodist Church. Bishop Gerald Kennedy, whose area includes Southern California and Arizona, sent the following telegram to Mr. Welch:

If you are doing anything more than spreading slander and suspicion, I invite you to meet at your convenience with the Board of Ministerial Training and Qualifications of The Methodist Church. I would like this board to tell you how we screen all men coming into our ministry and have you explain to us how any Communist could get through that screen. This board goes over a man's record from his birth with a fine-tooth comb. Furthermore, if you know of any man among the 734 ministers of the Southern California-Arizona Conference who are Communists or as you like to call them "comsymps" I would like to have you come before our Committee on Investigation and make your charge. The Methodist Church provides that any man who has anything against one of our preachers may make his accusations before this committee. The Methodist Church will act at once and if evidence is forthcoming, the accused will be brought to trial. If he is guilty, he will be dismissed from our ministry. I think it is about time that you get specific or else admit that you really do not know what you are talking about. Believe me, I am most anxious to have you come forth with any information you may have as I believe you will do if you are sincere.

As far as I know, Welch never responded to Bishop Kennedy's telegram.

Stance toward Negroes and Jews (in the West and Midwest)

With regard to the issue of religious, racial, or ethnic prejudice, the members of the Birch Society are torn in two directions. In the first place many of their members have such prejudices. But secondly, they know, and the unprejudiced members know, that to give these feelings and attitudes unbridled expression would lead to a labeling of the Birch Society as "racist" and this they perceive as fatal to such an organization. Therefore there are precautions taken to keep the expression of such sentiments of prejudice from the forefront. Welch, for example, devoted almost an entire *Bulletin* to a disclaimer of anti-Semitism. And further, a part of the justification given for the hierarchical authority to remove members from the home chapter and from local chapters is that of keeping the Birch Society clear of anti-Semites.

Anti-Negro prejudice is most characteristic of the older and the Southern-reared members of the Society whom I interviewed, but it is much less frequent among the middle-aged and younger members. As a group, however, the members interviewed were significantly more prejudiced than is our population as a whole.

On this issue of racial and religious prejudices, Welch himself deserves some real credit for his conduct. He has made and is making persistent efforts to keep the Birch Society clear of any trafficking in such prejudices. He is constantly faced with questions or accusations about alleged anti-Semitism that he or members of the Society might harbor. In my interviews with two of the Council members some evidence of anti-Semitism was discovered. But in both cases it was quite incidental to their major views. And there is fairly wide understanding and agreement with Welch's insistence that any anti-Semitism within the Society must be kept within strict bounds, that it must never develop to the point where it becomes the major preoccupation of a member or of a chapter.

There may have also been considerable pressure upon Welch to take an anti-Negro stand in the face of the movement toward complete desegregation and full civil rights. Such pressures would be particularly strong from the South and, with the drive toward equality of opportunity in housing, from the suburbs throughout the rest of the country. At this point Welch and the Society have been less forthright than on the question of anti-Semitism. They have taken the position that desegregation and civil rights are matters for the individual states not for the Federal Government. This is consistent with their general "states rights" position and with their antipathy toward "centralized" government. But it leaves them wide open to the charge that they are ignoring any effective guarantee of the individual rights and freedoms of an entire race of citizens within our country. This is a serious charge and Welch and his followers are stuck with it. For, to Welch's credit, he is not willing to take the segregationist's way out of this dilemma by claiming that Negro individuals are not really people.

Thus, the Birch Society is not racist in the sense that racism is a part of either its motivation or its goals. Its leaders and members recognize that overt racism is, in this country at this time (in the West and Midwest, if not in the Southeast), too far beyond the pale to be allowed to be a part of the Birch Society. For this reason, and because of Welch's outspoken opposition, religious, racial, and ethnic prejudices are suppressed.

Labor Unions and Big Business

The opinion constantly expressed by the Birch Society members I talked with was that labor unions were a good idea to begin with, but that their current leadership is bad. Interestingly enough, the distaste for these leaders centers more around a figure like Walter Reuther, who takes active leadership on political and economic issues, than around someone like Hoffa. But the esteem in which these same members hold big business is almost unqualified.

The Electorate

"The average individual has a basic respect for truth, but doesn't know what it is." To this view of the electorate, many Birch Society members would add, "and he's too apathetic to care." The electorate is viewed by many Society members as a great mass of voters controlled by either the left or the right. Too long, they feel, the left wing has been controlling these voters. It is now imperative that they be controlled by the right wing instead. Part of the role conceived by many leaders for the Birch Society is the "shocking" and "awakening" of these people "to what's really happening." The electorate, they feel, must be aroused from its apathy.

There is here an interesting parallel between political "apathy" and religious "sin." As much fervor is shown in a local chapter over a person who has "freed himself from apathy" and

who is now devoting all his (or her) awakened and renewed
energies to the "salvation" of "Americanism" and to the freeing of
others from the thralldom of "apathy" as there is among the
fundamentalists when one joins their number "freed from sin."

There is some, but not much, hope that the electorate can
be aroused from its apathy "in time." But underlying all of
these views there is a deep distrust of the electorate. This distrust
of their "majority rule," is the basic argument in Welch's contention that "this is a republic, not a democracy, let's keep it that
way."[7] The fear is that "majority rule" can change the laws
under which we are governed too quickly for the good of the
minorities or for our own "common weal." As Welch outlines
his argument, government under law is the distinctive and valua-
ble feature of a "republic." He grants that laws may be changed
but, with his distrust of the electorate's "majority rule," it is
unclear as to just who can legitimately do so. Presumably only
those deemed to be knowledgeable of the Communist conspiracy
and trustworthy in their opposition to it would he consider able,
legitimately, to change the laws of the republic.

Other Birth Society members take this same tack, holding
that only those who "know the issues" should be allowed to vote.

Civil Liberties

The Birch Society members interviewed agreed on the whole
that "It's the fellow travelers or Reds who keep yelling all the
time about civil rights." This suggests that many of them have
little respect for dissent and would tend to hold that "only truth
has rights." But a few with whom I talked were coming to a new
appreciation of the rights of dissent, especially in localities where
the Birch Society has been repudiated. Even while holding out
for "civil rights, not civil license," they were beginning to see the
necessity of the defense of civil liberties for at least their own
position on the political spectrum.

The Press

"How can we save our country if the press refuses to get
the word out to the people?" This is the lament of a Birch Society

member in Los. Angeles. Members of the Society feel that they have "The Truth" and they just do not understand why the press doesn't print it, radio and TV broadcast it, the schools teach it, churches preach it, and our government follow it.

Since the press doesn't (in most instances) print, without critical comment, the charges and analyses of the Birch Society, then, in the view of the Birchers, the press must be either blindly or willfully serving the Communists. They regard the press as overwhelmingly liberal, which is an interesting contrast to the view of most liberals that the press is overwhelmingly conservative. One member believes that 70 to 80 per cent of the working press is of liberal persuasion. Others go further, contending that the *Daily Worker* sets the "line" which is followed by the rest of the press two weeks later. An elaborate "case" for this explanation of Communist manipulation of the press has been built up around the "smear" of the Birch Society in early 1961.

Many members feel that you just can't believe the press. Consequently, the Birch Society and the rest of the American right wing feel they are reduced to "pamphleteering" and to dependence upon "reliable" right-wing publications. Such periodicals as *American Opinion,* the monthly *Bulletins* of the Birch Society, *Human Events,* and *The Dan Smoot Report* are highly regarded. To try to make these periodicals and anti-Communist books more widely available, the Birch Society has encouraged its members to open public reading rooms "that sell books." It even sends out a six-page manual advising how such "American Opinion Libraries" may be set up. They warn those who desire to set up such a reading room-bookstore that they should expect at least sixty days of deficit operation and they note that credit on books and periodicals that are ordered cannot be extended by the home office in Belmont for more than thirty days.

The spread of the Birch Society ideology is strongly dependent upon the availability of radically right-wing periodicals and books, which purport to present "documentation" of subversion by the Communists both internally and abroad. The establishment of reading rooms and patriotic bookstores, which abound in the Los Angeles area, for instance, has been a big factor in the spread, and particularly in the consolidation, of the ideological beliefs of the Birch Society.

Probably the biggest factor in the spread of this ideology, however, has been the various anti-Communist schools. These are held under many auspices. There were the military cold-war seminars sponsored by the military which were "muzzled" by Fulbright. There have been other local anti-Communist schools set up under the sponsorship of "Operation Alert," the "Cardinal Mindszenty Foundation," and the "National Indignation Convention," for example. And there are the schools sponsored in various places by Billy James Hargis of Tulsa and his "Christian Crusade." But perhaps the best known and the most highly organized are those set up by the "Christian Anti-Communist Crusade," led by Dr. Fred C. Schwarz, author of *You Can Trust the Communists (to be Communists)*.

Dr. Schwarz hits a city like a modern-day evangelist. Advance men and public relations experts prepare the way, mobilizing the support and obtaining the public endorsement of the leading political, business, professional, and religious figures of the area. Newspaper ads and spot radio and TV announcements prepare the populace. On opening night, in the largest auditorium available, with the endorsers crowded six deep on the platform and with a packed house, Schwarz steps into the range of the TV cameras and opens his "school."

The "school" usually lasts for at least one week and sometimes two. Once under way, it is in session morning, afternoon, and evening. A "faculty" of speakers, qualified by their dedicated anticommunism, carries most of the teaching load. Schwarz himself seldom speaks more than once a day. The lecturers on the "faculty" range from the dull to the exciting, but each discusses some aspect of the nature and the activities of the international Communist conspiracy—especially inside the United States.

"Tuition" paying "students" sit rapt day after day through the speeches and the occasional films. Some of those who work have been able so to plan their vacations that they can attend all the sessions. Besides the tuition, the schools derive other income from the sale of books, pamphlets, tracts, films, and tape recordings to students who wish to study more deeply or who wish to convert their friends or anathematize their enemies.

After a week or two of this anti-Communist "revivialism,"

Dr. Schwarz and his ever-changing "faculty" pack up their books, pamphlets, flags, and tape recordings and move on to the next town.

Such "schools" have done a great deal to stir up anti-Communist fervor, but few of them provide for any channeling of this excitement after they have left town. Interestingly enough, as early as the spring of 1961, Schwarz noted that, after he had left, Robert Welch often appeared to provide the "graduates" with a way to exercise their zealous anticommunism through the John Birch Society.[8]

Needless to say, such anti-Communist schools, with their presentation of an extremist and inflammatory ideology stir community conflict. And when the "graduates" are enrolled in the Birch Society, where the monthly *Bulletin* provides pipelines of information and directives, this conflict takes on an air of permanence.

Community Conflict—Birch Style

The character of the community conflict undertaken by local members of the Society is very distinctive; one cannot help but observe that it's more like warfare against a foreign enemy than like an argument with a neighbor. But it is accurate to say that a member of the Birch Society looks upon an opponent, even though he may live next door, as a representative of the Soviet Union. Thus, when a member of the Birch Society launches himself into the stream of conflict—over education, religion, labor unions, government, or whatever—the fray is wondrous to behold. And such conflict, no matter what issue may be at stake, is always defined as "Americanism *vs.* communism."

Former President Eisenhower seems to wade through this kind of fray and to shed attacks upon his motives and integrity without more than gritting his teeth. But such conflict on a more local level—across town or down the street—is not so easily shrugged off.

To understand why this is so, let us look through the eyes of a typical Bircher as he girds himself for such a fight. He is jubilant! He has, at last, found a local "Com Symp." (For the uninitiated, "com symp" is the supposedly nonslanderous label proposed by Welch for alleged "Communist sympathizers.") At last he can do his bit to plug the dike. The Com Symp in question has "tipped his hand." He has, perhaps only for an "unguarded" moment, shown his "true" colors. Even if he never does another thing to reveal his "true" Communistic sympathies, *anything* he does may be viewed through Welch's "principle of reversal," so that one can still "find the rascal out." And the members of the Birch Society that I interviewed were very quick to classify others as "enemies." And they are very close-minded about such "enemies" as well as about the ideological beliefs to which they have come.

Tone of the Conflict

Having once identified his prey, the only considerations a Bircher bothers with are those of strategy. He aims only to devise the most efficient means of exposure and destruction of his allegedly pro-Communist enemy. He feels no need to abide by any rules of civility or of rationality because he sees the enemy as so dangerous that such "formalities" cannot be tolerated. Therefore a Bircher moves to the attack, using methods that he would not condone under "more favorable" circumstances.

The Bircher's prey, having been hit below the belt in the first round of the conflict, usually responds in kind. Thus the battle becomes acrimonious at the outset, since each side views the other as seeking illegitimate goals by illegitimate means.

Conflict is nothing foreign to any of us. All of us have had differences of opinion and have been involved in arguments. All of us have also seen other individuals and groups do the same. Family arguments over bills, over who's going to use the car, over who won the last argument; community arguments over zoning for a new business or a new factory, over a school-board election, over the hiring or firing of a public official— such conflict is a normal and unavoidable part of social life. But the tone of such conflict usually starts at a fairly low pitch. It may get quite heated as it goes along, but at the beginning every-one's "polite" and "calm," observing the "rules." But not a member of the Birch Society—once they have "spotted" an opponent, all the rules are off.

Intent of the Conflict

Members of the Birch Society have little hope of converting their "Com Symp" opponent. They see this enemy person or group as so thoroughly "Un-American" that it's a waste of time to try to get them to reverse their position. Therefore the Birchers make no attempt to resolve points of disagreement. Instead they concentrate upon propagandistic efforts to win allies from the uncommitted public. For the public must be "alerted" and "mobilized" against the "evil" and "error" of the opposition and for the "goodness" and "truth" of their side. The American people must be made to see the Communist subversives in their midst.

The opponent of the Society may attempt to clarify and to resolve points of disagreement in the conflict. But when he discovers that the Bircher has no intention of "negotiating" and appears interested only in what the uncommitted public thinks—he, too, starts to try to find allies among the public.

In the more normal style of conflict to which most of us are accustomed, there is usually an effort to clarify and to resolve points of disagreement before "outsiders" are brought in. A husband and wife, when they first disagree, don't usually appeal to their neighbors. Contract negotiations between labor and management usually begin around a conference table rather than in full-page ads in the newspapers. The intent of most conflict is to clarify and resolve points of disagreement. But in Birch-style conflict differences are seen as total. They see no possible meeting of "communism" and "Americanism."

"Progress" and "Resolution" of the Conflict

Since there is no attempt by the Birchers to resolve issues, but only to engage in propagandistic charges and countercharges, the issues, charges, and countercharges tend to increase at nearly a geometric rate.

The opponents of the Society find themselves also enmeshed in this burgeoning conflict. There is, of course, no resolution of this kind of conflict through the ordinary settling of differences, which allows conflicting persons or groups to resume a workable relationship. For members of the Birch Society and their opponents, seeing each other's goals and means as wholly illegitimate, seeing each other as "Communists" and "Fascists," any such accommodation could be interpreted only as "appeasement." Nevertheless resolution of a sort does come to pass. It occurs as both sides are literally overcome by emotional strain as well as sheer weight and complexity of acrimonious and propagandistic charges. As both sides withdraw for a time to recoup their energies, and to prepare for the next fight, the conflict is temporarily "resolved" by being abandoned.

More normal conflict may well escalate in both its tone and in the number of issues at stake. A domestic argument over whose turn it is to take out the garbage may well be enlarged to include charges and countercharges over who's "letting down" in "all" responsibilities, over who's taking whom for granted; it may move to an icy discussion over custody of the children, and reach its climax as Dad takes out the garbage, slams the door, and goes downtown to bowl until two in the morning. A deadlock in labor management negotiations may lead to a lock-out or a strike, to angry charges and countercharges in the press, or to fist fights on the picket line. But most normal conflict—even though it may rise to a very high pitch and may come to include a great number of issues—is held within bounds and pulled toward resolution by ties of affection, trust, respect, rationality, civility, or, at the very least, by mutual interest. But the Bircher is devoid of feelings of affection, trust, or respect for his opponent. He feels unconstrained to observe the rules of either rationality or civility when dealing with what he believes to be a despicable traitor. The Bircher cannot even imagine any interests that might be shared by a "Communist" and an "Americanist," therefore any opponent of the Society becomes fair game in community conflict—Birch style.

Birch Society members may have much to contribute to public discussion of the great economic and political issues of our time, but their characteristic style of conflict—highly acrimonious, propagandistic, with no intent to resolve issues, which broadens rather than narrows, and which is "resolved" only as it falls of its own weight—obscures whatever these contributions might be and tends to lower all other conflict to the same level. Thus the political arena becomes more a battleground for shamen and tribesmen than a market place of ideas for free men.

CHAPTER VIII

But Before You Join . . .

The Relative Value of Sincerity

The most damning criticism that could be made of the members, and especially of the leaders, of the Birch Society would be to demonstrate that they're not sincere, thereby indicating that their proclaimed beliefs may be merely a smoke screen for what they're *really* after. But that does not appear to be the case among the members and the leaders of the Society that I have interviewed and observed. As a matter of fact, after Welch has allayed the apprehensions of an audience by explaining, with wry humor, that for that evening he has retracted his horns, probably the most compelling appeal he makes is that of his sincerity. For, in Welch, an audience sees a man who does not appear to be psychotic; who is obviously intelligent; who has, surprisingly enough, a sense of humor; and who is, above all, sincere. And sincerity, rather than rationality, is the garb with which most people in our country expect Truth to be clothed.

A rational discussion of truth is often suspect because of its complexity. This suspicion and rejection of unnecessarily obscure and occasionally arrogant rational discussion is one root of anti-intellectualism. A "sincere" presentation of what is called "truth," however, moves in the sphere of human emotion and is much more readily accepted. When we find the sincerity of a speaker to ring true, we often assume the same for his facts and his logic. Therein lies much of the appeal of Welch's "dynamic personal leadership."

But, unfortunately, rationality and sincerity are not necessarily related to each other. And here again we face the question of how conflicts are best to be resolved. There is no appeal besides force between two contradictory but equally sincere perceptions of truth. Such is not the case with rational perception of truth.

In rational conflict, the opposing parties have the opportunity to examine and question both the "facts" in contention and the way they have been used to build an argument. In the process, some "facts" are challenged and thrown out as untrue or irrelevant; other "facts" are often added until a conclusion is reached that is acceptable to both. Such rational debate is the only way which does *not* finally rely upon force to resolve conflict. Therefore we must conclude that rational debate is a very necessary part of a free and open society which we seek to maintain within this country. For if the rational handling of conflict is to become more widely accepted, if we as a people are to learn to rely upon something beyond "sincerity" and force to locate truth, then rational debate must be understood. The intellectuals of our country must be willing to abandon the obscure terminology of their special disciplines and to teach us by understandable words and actions how to resolve our conflicts in a rational manner.

The fact that the procedures and processes of rational conflict are not widely understood throughout our country accounts for the acceptance by so many people of an irrational ideology such as that of the Birch Society—and for the undue reliance upon sincerity alone as the test of truth. For, within our country generally, we have only one category of irrationality—that of mental illness. We thus find much of our society unprepared to deal critically with the irrational ideas of an apparently sane, intelligent, occasionally humorous, and always sincere spokesman like Robert Welch.

Some of the opponents of the Society would refuse to consider Welch, his followers, and their ideology as anything other than completely "paranoid" or "deviant." But by granting the possibility that the ideology of the Society may be rational, we can at least begin to bring the controversy surrounding this ideology away from the outer darkness of irrational conflict. Rational analysis is of value even if it's "unilateral."

The Basic Ideas Within the Ideology

Let us begin this rational analysis of the Birch Society ideology with a statement of the basic ideas set within the ideological framework through which members of the Society view social reality. As was said earlier, all economic and political data are modified to a greater or lesser degree by the content, by the rigidity or flexibility, and by the very existence of an ideological framework through which this reality must be viewed.

The basic ideas to which we now turn are fixed and unquestioned parts of the ideological framework of the Birch Society.

Bases of the Ideology in the Past and Future

A great deal of the argument of the Birch Society members is based upon their gleanings from "the lessons of history." These lessons are drawn primarily from Gibbon's *The Decline and Fall of the Roman Empire,* and have been reduced to an "oral tradition" that can be summarized as follows: Rome had a top-heavy governmental bureaucracy. It could gain political support by appealing to the masses with "bread and circuses." It could be supported financially only by taxing those within Rome who had enough "initiative" to meet their own financial obligations. The general provision of "bread and circuses" progressively undercut this spirit of financial "initiative" and progressively weaned individuals away from its practice. Therefore a downward spiral was set in motion in which the governmental bureaucracy systematically destroyed the financially responsible group upon which it was financially dependent. The application which a member of the Birch Society would make of this sort of a "lesson of history" is obvious in our contemporary society. But the truth of such lessons is suspect at two points. First, is this an accurate description and analysis of a historical event? In this example—the "fall of the Roman Empire"—the description and analysis is simplistic on the face of it. Historical events of this scope are just not explicable on the basis of one factor, and a student of ancient history would be quick to point out several other factors of equal importance. So, this description and analysis of an historical event is then suspect as to its accuracy. Secondly, such "lessons of history" are also suspect as to their contemporary applicability. There is serious question as to how much we can, in fact, learn from history, Santayana's statement that "those who refuse to learn from history are condemned to repeat it," notwithstanding. When one assumes that he can learn from history, he must still face honestly the question: "How much?"

Underlying the Birch Society's ideological interpretation of past, current, and future history is the basic pessimism of Spengler's *Decline of the West,* in which is envisioned a rigid cyclic growth and death of civilizations analogous to the seasons of spring, summer, fall, and winter. Mr. Welch explicitly repudiates Toynbee's more optimistic thesis of challenge-response as the work of "a meretricious hack."[1] Therefore, underlying the terrible parallels the Society members draw between our own and previous fallen civilizations, there is a more fundamental pessimism over the prospect of being unable to do much about the almost inevitable decay and death of our civilization.

Much of the ideology of the Birch Society is built upon the foundations of such "lessons of history." This discussion of them is designed simply to raise some fundamental questions as to the validity of these "lessons" which are presented as "self-evident truths."

The members of the Society also base a great deal of their ideological argument in the realm of future "consequences of political action." Of course any responsible political decision must include an anticipation of, at least, its immediate consequence. But such anticipation is extremely tenuous. Within the realm of political decisions, much of the power struggle centers around the publicly and privately anticipated immediate and long-range "consequences" of decisions. In evaluating the validity of any set of projected consequences of a decision, it is instructive to note that political opponents who seek an alternative or opposite direction for the decision in question are often able to muster a competing set of projected consequences fully as compelling and defensible. Many of these sets of projected consequences are, of course, based upon the "self-evident lessons of history"—the unimpeachable validity of which has already been called into question.

Not only do the analyses of projected consequences of current decisions differ, but also the analyses of the current consequences of past decisions. The analysis of the current consequences of the past decisions of the administration of Franklin D. Roosevelt is a pregnant case in point.

The analysis of the immediate consequences of our political decisions is, of course, of the utmost importance. In fact, it would seem that the direction of the national and international political decisions of our times will determine whether or not human life will continue on this planet. And, therefore, no one set among competing sets of projected immediate and longer-range consequences can safely be examined and accepted or rejected in isolation from the others. But it is precisely a presentation for acceptance or rejection of an isolated set of projected long-range consequences of contemporary political decisions that the Birch Society is attempting.

In the finding of "lessons from history," and particularly in the long-range projections of the consequences of current political decisions, there is, in fact, very little certainty for the conclusions to which one comes. Therefore, both areas abound in irrational conflict. For neither "lessons of history" nor the projected long-range consequences of political decisions can ever be held as rational certainties. They ought to be held as tentative hypotheses subject to rejection or modification by further evidence and by other competing tentative hypotheses. When they are held as dogmatic articles of faith instead of as tentative hypotheses they move conflict quickly to irrational levels.

Basic Presuppositions of the Ideology

In addition to these "background" ideas, there are four more presuppositions which are much nearer the forefront of the ideological framework of the Society:

1. Communism is the worst evil on the face of the earth. This is the underlying rallying point to "do something" about communism. Yet members of the Birch Society have only to mention it in passing because it has become so accepted within this country that it is almost a cliché

2. Capitalism has produced the greatest growth of civiliza-

tion to date—in terms of both material and (individualistic) personality values. This presupposition is very subsidiary to the first one on the unmitigated evil of communism, but its presence helps to explain the membership of a few otherwise moderate conservatives within the Society.

3. The course of history always hangs upon the conscious decisions of individuals or groups of men. Therefore any historical event can be traced to such a decision, the consequences of which are held to be foreseen and intentional. In other words, if anything goes wrong, someone is always to blame.

4. There is set a collision course between communism and capitalism. And because of the unqualified evil and unbending purposes of the Communists, there is no possibility that any modifications or any new synthesis can be brought about to avoid this collision.

The Central Syllogism

There is, in addition, a "central syllogism"—a core idea that has all the trappings of logic. This core idea builds upon the above presuppositions and gives them a turn which rests the blame for our losses to communism upon our "treasonable" national leaders. The syllogism runs as follows:

Communism is gaining power and influence daily over the world.

Our country was and is the most powerful nation in the world—yet our leaders have done and are doing nothing effective to stop this advance of communism.

Therefore—our national leaders must be consciously (or unconsciously) collaborating with (or allowing) the advance of communism.

The logic of the Birch Society begins to sound very compelling as we move into this analysis of their ideology. But it is well to remember that the truth of logical conclusions is dependent upon the accuracy of the facts upon which they are built. For instance, another logical syllogism might run: All men who attend Harvard are Communists. Robert Welch attended Harvard for two

years, therefore, Robert Welch is a Communist. The logic is perfect, but the conclusion is wrong—Robert Welch is not, as far as
I know, a Communist, though his "principle of reversal" would
identify him most clearly as a Communist. The conclusion is
wrong, not because the logic is faulty, but because some of the
facts are wrong. Obviously, "all men who attend Harvard" are not
Communists! Therefore, we must listen not only to the "sincerity"
and the "logic" of the "facts" presented by Robert Welch or anyone else. We must also ask whether each statement presented as a
"fact" is actually true. I have already raised such questions about
the validity of "lessons of history" and about the "certainty" that
particular long-range consequences will result from particular decisions—for instance, that the failure to impeach Chief Justice
Warren will insure that the Communists will be successful in
their efforts at internal subversion. (Those who combine a love of
Robert Taft, a hatred of Eisenhower, and a fear of Negroes seem
to make up the camp of those who would "buy" this long-range
projection.)

The presuppositions are also factually questionable. Welch
and his followers see Communists as completely evil; practically
everyone else in the world belongs to the human race, but not the
Communists. Is it factually correct that Communists are a sub-
human species with no ordinary human capacity for goodness?
Welch and his followers would agree, but others, especially those
from a truly evangelical Christian tradition, are not so ready to
dismiss the Communists from the human race. The other presuppositions are also all open to question, but discussion of them
would be too involved to undertake here.

The central syllogism is also factually questionable. There is
considerable debate about the continuing growth of communism,
and in its growth to date it is far from unified. It is widely accepted that our country is the most powerful in the world. And we
have tried and continue to try various means of halting and
reversing the unquestionable growth that the Communists have
achieved. The members of the Birch Society are noisy in their
criticism of these efforts, but the alternatives they propose would
lead us either toward complete isolation from the Communists or
toward total war with them. Our engagement of the Communists

has to be both more realistic and less foolhardy than this. Therefore, since the "facts" of the syllogism are questionable, so is the
"logic" of its conclusion, which mistakenly sees our national leaders as conscious collaborators with the Communists.

One further point—let's look once more at the conclusion
of that syllogism on a more pedestrian level. Let's look at our
local high-school basketball team instead of at our nation. And
let's say that this team seemed destined for the state championship.
Once again the syllogism: Our arch-rival from the next town is
beating us. But ours was and is the best basketball team in the
state, yet the players are losing. *Therefore,* the coach and the
players on the team must be "throwing" the games with our rival.
Following this logic, the "Birch Society Boosters Club" will insist
on using basketball practice sessions to "grill" the coach and the
first string in an effort to locate the "traitors." The absurdity of
this one-track-minded ideology is immediately apparent. It completely ignores the possibility that the team might better spend its
time sharpening their plays, scouting their opponents, and even
improving their passing and shooting.

Additional Beliefs

For good measure, the members of the Birch Society add
other beliefs which serve partly to round out their ideology and
partly to "protect" it from change. Whenever their ideology is
threatened, they seem more ready to add additional beliefs than
to consider changing any of their former beliefs. Thus the ideology
of the Birch Society tends to become more and more "logic-tight,"
more and more impervious to change.

1. All advances of communism must be stopped and re-
versed.

2. We have effective political leverage only within our own
country. Therefore, we must purge the leadership of our government and all of our other institutions of persons with ideas which
lead them to promote or tolerate communism or anything related
to it. Then we will be equipped to meet unified and centrally

organized communism with our unified, centrally organized, and innately superior economic-political "American way of life."

3. If you're not 100 per cent with the Birch Society in what they perceive to be the "central conflict of our age," then you are considered in the Communist camp. If you're not 100 per cent against communism—in their terms—then you're for it.

4. All peripheral conflict is disruptive of the unity we need to meet the central conflict with communism. Therefore all those who foment conflict or who make criticisms of our country (besides Birch Society members) are perceived as Communist agents or unwitting dupes. There is only the one basic conflict (an apocalyptic view), and that is between the "good" of "the American way of life" and the "evil" of communism. All conflict not directly related to this central conflict drains off energies that would be better used within it.

5. All news of both domestic and international matters is seen to be related to this central conflict. Therefore a member of the Society reads and listens to reporters and interpreters of events to see on which side they stand in this conflict. Once a reporter, or interpreter, or a participant "tips his hand"—that is, is seen as having a Communistic "spot or blemish"—then everything he does thereafter is seen as his part within the total Communistic conspiracy. If the statements and actions of this individual (or group) don't always—or ever—thereafter seem to identify him clearly as a conscious agent of the Communist conspiracy, there are only two alternatives. He may be a witless "dupe," or he may be more clever than he seems to be. In this view, he is seen as trying to cover his tracks so that he may maintain his place of influence or gain a higher one so that he can become a more effective agent of the Communist conspiracy. Therefore you apply Welch's "principle of reversal" and ferret him out. That is, once one is suspect, then even actions which appear to be directed against the Communists are merely "cover-ups." If one is suspect, therefore, *anything* he does confirms all the suspicions that a Bircher has of him. This "principle of reversal" is also applied to an interpretation of Soviet foreign policy. Any overtures from the Soviet Union (or any Communist state) about disarmament, peaceful coexistence, or

any other "superficially" attractive proposal, is perceived by the Birchers as a "smoke screen" serving other ulterior motives.

Lining up the Sheep and the Goats

How then does a person or a group become suspect? Let us push this question back to a more basic level. How do all of us go about classifying one another into friendly, neutral, or enemy camps? Robert Chin, a professor of Social Psychology at Boston University, suggests that there is a pattern into which all such classification fits. This pattern can be described as a chain with five links, diagramed as follows:

Link One: What KIND OF PERSON OR GROUP is this? These "friends," "enemies," or "neutrals" may be described in a vast number of ways—the following are only a few examples: Communist, Socialist, Anarchist, Baptist, Methodist, Pacifist, Rightist, Leftist, Conservative, or Militarist.

Link Two: What are their IDEOLOGICAL BELIEFS? What is their background of education, family, and thought which gives an indication or an explanation of their ideological beliefs?

Link Three: Their INTENTIONS. What consequences do they "intend" their actions to have?

Link Four: Their ACTIONS. What do they do?

Link Five: What are the CONSEQUENCES of their actions—as observed and interpreted—as anticipated?

We classify persons or groups according to what we can discover, observe, or infer about their "ideological beliefs," their motivating "intentions," their "actions," and the "consequences" of their actions. We all move up and down this chain of classification inferring missing links from known links. For example, we often infer that someone "intended" that his "action" have the "consequences" that it did. This is the moot point, for example, in a first-degree murder trial as a jury tries to decide whether the defendant "intended" beforehand to kill another. When we try to figure out whether a person who's "not saying" is a Democrat, a Republican, or a Bircher, for another example, we draw inferences from his educational and family background about his "ideological beliefs," from his "actions" as we can observe them, from his "intentions" as we understand them, and from the "consequences" of his actions as we gauge and evaluate them.

An extremely open-minded person characteristically demands evidence from two or more links, the classification he arrives at is always tentative, never closed.

A person with an extremely closed mind first looks for any evidence at any point along the chain, and the classification he arrives at is final.

A typical and contemporary example distinguishing between those of an open or closed mind would be their perception of a person who signed a petition (an "action") backing a cause which is later demonstrated to be in the enemy camp. The person with an extremely closed mind would take this to be "tip-off" enough and would permanently classify the offender as in the enemy camp. The person with an extremely open mind would note this "action," but would wonder if the offender "intended" his action to have the "consequences" that it did—whether the person was, in this, acting from the center of his "ideological beliefs" or whether the action represents a minor aspect of them—and whether the offender is really the "kind or person" that this one action might superficially lead one to classify him to be. The extremely open-minded person would demand further evidence before he was willing to give the offender a tentative classification. But, as we said, the extremely closed-minded person would find one bit of evidence enough to consign the offender into a permanent classification. If future evidence seemed to contradict this initial classification, the person with a closed mind would ignore it, add some "additional beliefs," or apply some sort of "logical principle," such as Welch's "principle of reversal," in order to bend even contradictory evidence to support his initial classification of the offender.

The *Blue Book,* and the other literature of the Birch Society abounds with closed-minded "documentation" indicating that other persons, groups, or nations are Communistic. The statement of the ideology, especially as it moves to build its case "documenting" internal subversion, is typically closed-minded—deduc-

ing from fragmentary evidence of one of these links of classification, background, intention, action or consequences, all the
others. In its classification of persons and groups, the ideology of
the Birch Society comes very close to being a "pure" example of
a closed-minded ideology.

The Closed-Minded Ideology

Not only is the Birch Society ideology itself of the closed-
minded type, it is also held in a closed-minded way by the Birch
Society leaders and members I interviewed.[2] The distinction
drawn by the psychologist Milton Rokeach between open- and
closed-minded persons centers upon their ability or inability to
evaluate information as true or false purely upon its own merits.
The completely closed-minded person is incapable of doing this.
He can judge the truth or falsity of information only by its
source; he is utterly lost in the market place of ideas.

We have already spoken of how most members of the Birch
Society classify other persons and groups. They are very slow to
classify a person or a group as an ally and very quick to classify
a person or a group as an enemy. But once such a classification is
made, any and all information from that person or group is accepted or rejected according to whether they've been classified as
an ally or as an enemy. For the extremely closed-minded person,
no information or supposed "facts" are evaluated on their own
merits. He carefully selects an intellectual trough, but then he eats
anything that is dumped before him.

The major characteristics of those described by Rokeach as
dogmatic and closed-minded are three. First of all, as we have
said, such persons have difficulty in separating information from
its source. They are unable to evaluate information on its own
merits. Second, such persons see the world as threatening and, because of their difficulty in separating information from its source,
seek certainty through reliance upon authority. This reliance upon
the security and certainty of authority, in turn, heightens their
original difficulty in separating information from its source. Third,
Rokeach believes that all persons have "two opposing sets of

motives—the need to know and the need to defend against threat."[3] But, even as the dogmatic, closed-minded person seeks to "defend" himself and his ideological beliefs against a world perceived as threatening, he can gain psychological satisfaction of his motive to "know" by "mastering" all the information fed to him by his chosen authority. These characteristics of the closed mind are exhibited to a high degree by the members and leaders of the Birch Society—they choose Robert Welch as their major authority and most of them accept information that he feeds to them without question. Goldwater is O.K., too. But just see how far Eisenhower, or Rockefeller, or Warren, or Nixon get when they try to set forth some information. None of them are acceptable authorities for the members of the Birch Society—and I'm sure all of them are quite happy to hear it.

But before "liberal" readers get too complacent and "conservative" readers get too upset, I should tell them that Rokeach finds the open and closed mind to be independent of political affiliation. That is, though an extremist of either the right or the left is most apt to be closed-minded, closed-minded persons are to be found among the "liberals" and "middle-of-the-roaders" in as great numbers as among the "conservatives."

To summarize, we began this analysis and criticism of the ideology of the Birch Society by noting the sincerity of its leaders and members, but we pointed out that there is not necessarily any relationship between sincerity and an accurate perception of reality. Following this observation we examined the basic beliefs of the ideology. The careful reader will have noted the neat internal logical consistency of these ideological beliefs and the defenses provided against their modification, as well as the doubtful validity of many of these beliefs. Thus the ideological beliefs of the Society are vulnerable, within the arena of rational conflict, because of the failure of the members of the Society to allow for their correction and modification, but this failure itself is due to the closed-minded inability of the members of the Society to assess the validity of the criticisms of "outsiders." In addition to this "logic-tight" character of their ideological beliefs, both their closed-minded classification of other persons and groups, and their closed-minded inability to separate information from the sources so classified contribute to the rigid and rationally invulnerable character of the total ideological framework of the Birch Society.

The Appeals of the Society

What attracts members to the Society? Why have many prominent businessmen and other leaders chosen to follow Welch? What are the appeals?

The fundamental social strain to which the Birch Society makes an appeal is, of course, hatred of and fear of communism. But the Birch Society also appeals to those especially affected by other social-psychological strains within our country. These strains can be broadly identified as anomie,[4] dispossession of power and status, particularly for those once powerful in business, governmental, military and economic decision-making,[5] and placement within the age and sex structure in our country in an "insignificant" role such as that of housewife or of male unemployment in retirement.[6] The appeal to strains such as this would, however, be present in nearly every movement of protest. The distinctive appeal of the Birch Society is to be found in its ideology.

The base for certainty: We are in a social setting characterized by hatred of communism, by anomie, and by extensive alteration of our social structure. In such a social setting, one of the major appeals of the rigid and invulnerable ideology of the Society is in its provision of a base for certainty. The ideology of the Society provides certainty of understanding because it is a fairly simple framework of interpretation through which to view world and national events. It offers additional certainty to Society members as its authority figures, Welch and others, continually provide the members with "deeper" and "broader" understanding of what's "really" going on in the world and within our country. Thus the very simplicity, rigidity, and authority for the ideology all help provide a "believer" with this certainty of understanding. And he is also provided with courses of action which, undertaken in concert with many other members, under the direction of a broadly accepted "dynamic personal leader," reinforce certainty of understanding with assurance that "something" at last is being done.

One reason why the framework of the ideology is so strongly protected and defended is that it provides this certainty of understanding and direction.

The perception of self-righteousness: Psychologically the
ideology provides its members with the gratifying feelings of self-
righteousness at being on the "right" side in "the central conflict
of our age." This also serves to override any sense of guilt for
personal sins by providing members of the Society with this
same assurance that they are on the right side on the "really"
important issues. The sense of guilt for said sins is also often
handled by convenient ideological "rationalizations." For example,
employers who wish to drive wages down and profits up
can do so through promotion of so-called right-to-work legislation. But they can allay any feelings of guilt they might have
over this by proclaiming to others that they're "really" defeating
collectivist communism. Thus, the belief in the ideology of the
Birch Society serves to provide its members with a sense of self-
righteousness.

The perception of superiority: Being on the "right" side provides members as well with a perception of themselves as superior
to those on the "wrong" side. They can thus feel superior to opponents with higher educational attainment and higher social
status. In this sense the ideology presents a low-status, dispossesed,
or otherwise disdainfully regarded member of the Society with
psychological upward social mobility at least within his own mind.

These social-psychological appeals of certainty of understanding and direction within an uncertain world, and the perception of
self-righteousness and superiority are some of the same appeals
offered by a religious sect. Not only does acceptance of the
ideology of the Birch Society offer these attractive social-psychological appeals; it also offers the opportunity "justifiably" to direct
the aggression arising from frustration toward the person or group
who caused this frustration. It is possible to retaliate with such
aggression not only toward those of lower power and social status,
but toward those of higher as well. This is fundamentally different from the usual modes of expression of aggression. Ordinarily
when a person of higher power and status creates frustration for

one of lower status, the aggression must be displaced; it cannot be directed toward the object of frustration.[7]

"Justified" aggression: Backed by the Society's ideology, aggression is not displaced. In the name of Americanism, it is directed toward those otherwise invulnerable sources and objects of frustration. Thus when a member or leader of the Society classifies an act, its intent, or its consequences as that of a Communist sympathizer frustrating "true Americanism," then the person or group in question is "justifiably" subject to attack by these members or leaders of the Society. The basic mechanism of frustration-aggression described by Allport almost always runs as follows when it is confronted with a much more powerful object of frustration: frustration → aggression → displacement.[8] But the ideologically modified mechanism of the Birch Society runs as follows despite the nature of the object of frustration: ideological definition of frustration → aggression → ideologically "justified" irrational conflict with the object of frustration. The ideological framework of the Birch Society, through which frustration is perceived, incites the Birch Society to aggression and nerves it for irrational conflict with all sources and objects of frustration. Such objects and sources are identified in two ways: through identification by the Birch Society and through identification of themselves as they rise in conflict against the Society. For by rising in opposition to the Birch Society, a person or a group is, in the perception of members of the Society, self-identified as a Communist agent or dupe.

Thus the distinctive, ideologically modified frustration-aggression mechanism of the Birch Society becomes one of the social-psychological appeals of the ideology, since it provides for release of frustration directly against the source or object or real or imagined frustration.

In summary, the ideology of the Birch Society leads its members to express their aggressions directly against the sources of their frustration in the form of irrational conflict and in a mood of certainty, self-righteousness, and superiority. Therein lie its social-psychological appeals. Because of the psychological satisfactions offered by these appeals, it is almost impossible to "wean" a member away from the logic-tight and closed-minded ideology of the Birch Society.

CHAPTER IX

Postscript and Conclusions: 1966

Many things have happened to the John Birch Society since this book was published in the spring of 1964, but the November, 1964, defeat of Senator Barry Goldwater, the Republican candidate for President, has been the central fact for the Society since that time—the origin of both its growth and its broadening repudiation.

Though not sharing their conspiratorial view of history, Senator Goldwater had seemed to the Society a knight in shining armor. Many of the members affirmed the ideological "purity" of what they saw as his views on free enterprise versus federal controls and on states rights versus civil rights. And the Birch Society had finally received its long-sought blessing of respectability when, in his acceptance speech, Goldwater had maintained that "extremism in the defense of liberty is no vice." The Birchers got the message and were jubilant. Other conservative and moderate Republicans got the message, too, and became heartsick as they witnessed the polarization of their party and the shattering defeat of the already weakened half of our two-party system.

In the wake of that disastrous 1964 presidential election, Republicans have been taking a second look at the Birch Society. In its October 19, 1965, issue, the editors of William Buckley's conservative *National Review* devoted an entire series of articles to "The John Birch Society and the Conservative Movement."

Noting that the Birch Society had opened a major campaign to recruit new members, the editors of the *National Review* commented that many of the Birch materials being used in the campaign were misleading. For instance, a Birch Society Sunday supplement magazine published in many major cities carried a picture of former president Eisenhower, and a text that seemed to say that he approved of the John Birch Society—even though Robert Welch continues to believe that Eisenhower is a Communist.

The *National Review* editors also felt that the Birch Society had reached, during the summer of 1961, a new level of virulence and panic. And to footnote that observation, they pointed to the July-August, 1965, "Scoreboard" issue of *American Opinion* in which it was said that the United States is now "60–80%" Communist-dominated.

To point up the gravity of these activities of the Birch Society, the editors of *National Review* noted that

Political contests of major significance are coming up involving important anti-Communist conservatives—for instance, Senator John Tower's campaign in Texas, and Ronald Reagan's campaign for the governorship of California—in which the John Birch Society will figure. It is important to win victories in Texas and California—and elsewhere; and important, therefore, to raise the question explicitly whether the activities of Mr. Robert Welch and of some of the members of the John Birch Society are at the margin helpful to such men as Tower and Reagan, or hurtful to them.

Continuing the *National Review* analysis of the relationship between the Birch Society and the conservative movement, there is a reprint of a syndicated column of William Buckley, the unsuccessful anti-Lindsay candidate for Mayor of New York, in which he notes that for years there have been those who have defended the Birch Society as a "fighting organization devoted to anti-socialism and anti-Communism" and who have maintained that the "unfortunate conclusions" which Robert Welch had drawn about President Eisenhower in 1958 should be ignored when one assessed the Birch Society of the present day. Mr. Buckley finds himself in strong disagreement with this position and said, "I regret to say that it is in my judgment impossible to defend the leadership of the John Birch Society if one reads closely even its contemporary utterances."

Then Mr. Buckley goes on to catalogue some of these utterances which had appeared in the July-August, 1965 "Scoreboard" issue of *American Opinion,* an issue which sought to "document" the claim that the United States was now "60–80%" under Communist domination.

The activities of the Communists in all fields appear to the Birch Society to be designed "to kill loyalty to the United States, respect for the white race, comprehension of Western civilization, and veneration of God." The editors of *American Opinion* go on to note ominously that "simultaneous movement in a hundred different supposedly unrelated segments of our national life cannot be mere coincidence."[1] The "documentation" of such claims, to which Mr. Buckley objected so strongly, included statements such as the following: Mental health* is singled out for its role in this "simultaneous movement."

The attention of the American people was first drawn to the real problem of "mental health" on October 1, 1962, when, in obedience to the specific demands of the Communist Party, a gang under the direction of Nicholas Katzenbach (now Attorney General of the U.S.) kidnaped General Edwin A. Walker in Oxford, Mississippi . . .[3]

Medicare also, it appears, is a part of the plan. It seems that

. . . the principal object of "Medicare" is to destroy the independence and integrity of American physicians; it will inevitably create a "pressing shortage" of physicians and nurses. Communist provinces are sure to have a surplus . . . they will be glad to export to the United States to relieve the "shortage."[4]

Civil Rights occupies a key position in the minds of the editors of *American Opinion*. For instance, in Selma, ". . . a horde of termites from all over the country, led by half-crazed ministers and professors, swarmed over the small town of Selma, Alabama, in a typical demonstration of Communist activism."[5] Further along in the article it is stated that

. . . the enemies of mankind were able to whip up such hysteria among the

---

* It is of interest to note a strain of preoccupation with sexual perversions in this "Scoreboard" article—the focus of the Birch Society almost shifts from the international Communist conspiracy to some sort of international homosexual conspiracy.[2]

brainwashed and the unthinking that Congress was somehow bullied into doing what, in the opinion of all observers in Washington, it never would have done, had Kennedy remained alive. It enacted the "Civil Rights Act," which, as Ezra Taft Benson warned, "is part of the pattern for the Communist takeover of America."[6]

Of the Supreme Court, the Birch Society maintains that "the theory that the Warren Court is working for a domestic, as distinct from foreign, dictatorship becomes less tenable every day."[7]

Regarding the government as a whole, the Birch Society believes that "as Communist control is extended through all branches of our government, we can expect increasing use of governmental powers to harass, persecute, and, where possible, ruin Americans who openly disapprove of the Communist takeover of their country."[8]

After simply quoting a series of statements like the foregoing from the leadership of the Birch Society, Mr. Buckley wonders "how it is that the membership of the John Birch Society tolerates such paranoid and unpatriotic drivel."[9]

That initial column drew considerable response from the membership of the Society. The vitriolic character of that response led Mr. Buckley to raise, in a second column, two additional questions.

One: Is there in fact substantial disagreement between the membership at large, and the leadership of the JBS? Two: Do the members of the JBS make any attempt to understand what it is that the leadership of the JBS believes; or do they simply ignore the zanier findings of the leadership, taking shelter in the argument that the Society is anti-Communist, and that therefore all anti-Communists should support it?

And the editors of the *National Review* agreed that "the John Birch Society, as headed by Mr. Robert Welch, is a grave liability to the conservative and anti-Communist cause."

The *National Review* printed several letters commending Mr. Buckley for the series of columns. Among them were letters from Russell Kirk and Senator John Tower.

Barry Goldwater also took the opportunity to express a somewhat chastened view of the Birch Society and of its leadership. He wrote in part:

> I have, on several occasions, suggested that if the present leadership of this Society were to, in the best interests of the Society, withdraw and have the group select new leaders, a great deal of their trouble would disappear . . .
>
> I don't for one moment agree with some Republican leaders that this organization is about to take over the Republican Party, but I do believe that the type of people generally who I know as members of the group, could add effective weight and work to the Republican Party if they cared to, but they should resign from the Society, since Mr. Welch has declined to do so.

Other Republican leaders are certainly concerned about the possibility of a Birch Society takeover of substantial portions of the Republican Party.

Senator Thruston B. Morton, the Senate GOP campaign chairman and a former Republican national chairman, was widely quoted when he said in September, 1965, that he was truly concerned about a "precinct-by-precinct" takeover of the GOP organization by Birch Society members. He recalled the fact that "organized labor and the Democratic Party kicked out the Communists when they tried to infiltrate those groups. We've got to do the same thing with the Birchers." Senator Morton went on to say, "I want to see us kick the John Birch Society right square in the tail. I think it is as dangerous as the Ku Klux Klan and the Communist Party."

Senator Morton said that the need for action was made more urgent by the fact that the Society, with Reed Benson (son of former Agriculture Secretary Ezra Taft Benson) in charge, had opened a Washington office to press its cause. Thruston Morton concluded by saying that: "I've laughed off the Birch Society in the past—I've taken Barry Goldwater's line that there were more Democrats in it than Republicans. Now it's time to do something."[10]

Other Republican leaders quickly joined in the attack.[11] Senate Minority Leader Everett M. Dirkson said: "They are not a part of the Republican Party, they never have been and they never will be." And he added that: "In the American political scheme, I do not think there is any place or any room for an organization that operates on a secret basis to achieve its political goals."

Senator Jacob Javits noted that the Birch issue within the party has been clear: ". . . at least since the 1964 convention when a floor resolution denouncing it failed. From what I see, a similar resolution would succeed today."

Enlarging upon his remarks of the previous day, Senator Morton observed that Senator John Tower of Texas had to fight the Society in the Houston area, Governor Daniel Evans of Washington had the same problem and that Governor George Romney of Michigan had a "knock-down-drag-out" with the Society.

How has the Birch Society responded to this widespread repudiation? Predictably. Founder Robert Welch believes that the statements by leaders of the conservative movement and the Republican Party are prompted not by their concern over what is best for the Republican Party and for the country, but by clandestine orders from the conspiracy. Welch does grant that "most" of the attack against himself and the Society "is by good people who have no idea that somehow they have been beguiled into carrying the ball for the Communists and doing the comrades' dirty work."[12] Welch goes on to say rather somberly to his members that "There is nothing on earth which could show you so well and so convincingly the extensiveness and depth now reached by the Communists influences in this country as the depth and extensiveness of the present attack on ourselves."[13]

The Birch Society, then, has become a divisive and weakening influence within the Republican Party and has served as an invitingly vulnerable "straw man" for those liberals who wish to avoid debate on issues raised by conservatives. Consequently, the John Birch Society and Robert Welch have been increasingly repudiated in the sphere of party politics.

But members of the Birch Society have been active in other fields.

Public Schools

The public schools have been under continuing attack since this book was first published in 1964. One main focus of the attack

by the Birch Society has been upon local Parent-Teachers Associations. Apparently a directive by Robert Welch to members of
the Society in the September, 1960, *Bulletin* has begun to be carried out by zealous followers in a number of cities and towns. In
that *Bulletin,* Welch urged his followers:

Join your local P.T.A. at the beginning of this school year, get your conservative friends to do likewise, and go to work to take it over. You will
run into real battles, against determined leftists who have had everything
their own way. But it is time we went on the offensive . . .

This initial directive by Welch created such a furor in the
press that members apparently did not wish to pursue such infiltration right away. But since September, 1960, there had been
enough years for the heat to die down—and there had also been a
hard-fought presidential primary and election campaign. And
many Birch Society members have now equipped themselves with
the parliamentary savvy, with the nerve, and with the necessary
amount of "true Americanism" for such infiltration and takeover.

In the course of such a takeover, the parliamentary infighting often becomes intense. As Ernest Dunbar reported in *Look*:

In some PTA meetings, attempts are made to prolong discussion,
frequently by the injection of irrelevant issues so that weary parents will
depart in disgust and an important vote can be taken in their absence.
Another gambit is to pack a nominating committee with "ultraconserva-
tives." And when a slate is nominated with extremists in all key positions,
moderates in their alarm often add to the nominations a host of their
candidates. Comes the vote, the moderate ballots are split among many
moderate candidates and the extremists' ballots are cast for the extremist
candidates brought in by the ultraconservative nominating committee.[14]

Often the object of the takeover of a local P.T.A. is to get it
to withdraw from the state and national P.T.A. organizations.
The ire of many members of the Birch Society is aroused by the
P.T.A.'s endorsement of Federal aid to education and equal-op-
portunity civil rights legislation. In addition to undercutting support of these policies, a Birch Society takeover of a local P.T.A.
can also provide a very good beachhead from which to attack "pro-

Communist" teachers or textbooks. If school administrators resist this kind of purge of teachers, texts, and course offerings, such a local P.T.A. group can then exert pressure for the election of a "truly Americanist" school board to deal with such "personnel problems." Birchers and others have come to realize that since so few people generally turn out for school board elections, it is an easy task to win such elections through a determined, carefully-planned campaign. Just such a Birch Society dominated school board was elected in Pleasantville, Iowa.[15] The result was that the Superintendent of Schools was forced to resign and nineteen of the town's thirty-four teachers resigned in protest. Many towns-people now ruefully admit that they were "asleep at the last election." This was not an isolated case.

Get US Out . . . of Viet Nam

One of the more bizarre logical swerves of Welch's "principle of reversal" lines him up with the teach-ins, demonstrations, draft card burnings, and self-immolations in a united demand to "Get US out of Viet Nam." "Get US Out" used to be reserved for the Birch Society drive to get us out of the United Nations. For those who are at least mildly surprised that this slogan now applies equally to Viet Nam, Welch in the *Bulletin* for August, 1965, said that: "We knew exactly what we were saying, *and were looking ahead to this kind of situation,* when we first coined the phrase: Get US out!"

To follow Robert Welch through his logical labyrinth, it is only fair that he speak for himself. Welch begins with the incredulous question:

What on earth is the matter with our compatriots in the American anti-Communist movement, anyway? The Communists, by exercising a minimum of discipline and of control by propaganda, over a relatively few thousand beatniks and halfbaked collegiate brats, and by passing the word to a few of their highly placed agents, create a leftwing demand that the United States pull out of Vietnam! And this gambit fools the American people into thinking that we are serving some purpose, other than exactly what the Communists want, by what we are doing in Vietnam! Naturally the Communists have been doing everything they could to advance the theme that it is our patriotic and humanitarian duty to "stand firm" in Vietnam, and to keep on increasing our forces and our involvement there as the war is "escalated"—exactly according to their plans—into a greater Korea. . . .

* * *

Unless some way can be found to upset and reverse these plans, which the Communists are imposing on this Administration and carrying out through this Administration, you are going to see more and then many more American boys dying in southeast Asia, to support the Communist propaganda that the United States is a paper tiger whose tail can be twisted with impunity. You are going to see all remaining American prestige in eastern Asia, and all will to resist Communism on the part of the patriotic natives of that whole area, both completely destroyed. And far more important than either, in the long run, you are going to see the fact that we are at war used increasingly and ever more brazenly, to enable the Communists in government, in the press, in the pulpit, and in every other division of our national life, to label all criticism of their captive Administration as treasonous. You will see that Administration begin to establish controls over the lives and actions of the American people which will make all of the regimentation we have had so far look like a study in free enterprise; and begin suppressing all opposition by the usual Communist police-state methods.

* * *

So we say *Get US out!*, and add no ifs or buts. From the very time the slogan was first conceived, we have recognized the possibility that there might be those in due course who would interpret it broadly, as follows:

"Get us out of this whole foreign worldwide mess in which we are playing so cruel and so ignominious a part, and let's clean up all of the crime and dirtiness and deficits and moral debauchery here at home." But we have no objection to this meaning. We still simply say, as emphatically as we can: *Get US out!*[16]

* * *

Civil Rights

Racial bigotry, shamed by Selma, rediscovered its own warped justification in Watts. And the Birch Society immediately seized upon this turn of events. Emblazoned across the front of the September, 1965, *Bulletin* was the call, "Fully expose the 'civil rights' fraud and you will break the back of the Communist Conspiracy." It was now possible for the Birch Society to direct its membership drive much more fully and much more openly to the more "respectable" of the Southern segregationists and to the irritated white "backlasher" now suddenly fearful, in the North and in the West. These two groups have been the sources from which the Birch Society has drawn its most recent membership gains.

Following the 1964 election, coordinators from the Birch Society moved into many areas of significant Goldwater strength. But the appeal of the Birch Society to segregationists and white backlashers extends beyond those who were disappointed in their backing of Goldwater. Birch Society billboards calling for Chief Justice Earl Warren's impeachment have stood along Southern highways for some time now. Warren has been seen by many Southerners as the chief architect of the civil rights movement ever since the Supreme Court handed down its school desegregation decision in 1954. So the Southern segregationist makes his own calculation rather quickly—any outfit that's an enemy of Warren is a friend of mine!

A further appeal to segregationists and white backlashers has blossomed out of what appeared to be the rather prosaic Birch Society campaign to "Support Your Local Police" which was initiated in the *Bulletin* for July, 1963. The main point of this campaign seems to be that the local police are to be supported particularly in their handling of civil rights demonstrations. Charges of "police brutality" are to be almost automatically discounted, and calls for the establishment of civilian review boards are to be resisted. For the Birch Society sees both as Communist-inspired attempts to hamstring and to discredit local enforcement so that it can be replaced by a Communist-dominated centralized police force "like . . . the 'federal marshals' used in Mississippi."[17] For anyone who missed the double message, the *Bulletin* for November, 1965, carries a full page picture of Alabama's Governor Wallace, surrounded by a pleasant enough appearing seventeen-man Alabama Committee To Support Your Local Police, signing the proclamation for an official Support Your Local Police Week in his state—the only thing missing from the picture are chained and snarling police dogs. On the next page of that *Bulletin,* Welch is also glad to share news of another happy occasion—it seems that Sheriff James G. Clark, widely known for his work in Selma, Alabama, has just been honored by his election as First Vice President of the National Sheriff's Association, a group with a membership of about 20,000.[18]

Many rabid Southern segregationists and resentful, fearful, Northern or Western white backlashers know that they have found a home in the John Birch Society. Within its ranks they may occasionally be chided when they speak of Negroes in profane and derogatory terms, but they will always be encouraged to excoriate the "Communists" who are running our present Administration and the "Communists" who are leading the civil rights movement. And they can also engage in action programs that help "keep the Negro in his place" by pressing the campaign to impeach Earl Warren, by supporting their local police, and by seeking to discredit the motivation and the aims of every law, every judicial decision, and every leader seeking to secure the guarantee of liberty and justice for all.

Those who think they see something of significance in the current interest of the John Birch Society in the local police should see a letter reprinted in the November, 1965, issue of the *Bulletin*. Written by the Department of the Air Force in Washington, it was in response to an inquiry about membership of Air Force personnel in the John Birch Society. The letter stated in part:

> The United States Air Force has no policy regarding this society and neither encourages nor discourages membership therein. However, participation in outside organizations may not interfere with the full performance of military duties nor contravene existing law or regulation.
>
> We therefore take no official position toward the John Birch Society.

The only comment from the editors of the *Bulletin* to this photostatic document was: "There are many letters like the above on record, from all departments of the armed forces."[19]

The Present State of the Society

This postscript chapter has indicated some of the new directions being taken by the Society—stronger, more frequent, and more sophisticated attacks upon public education; a very unexpected position on Viet Nam; and a disturbingly racist attitude toward the civil rights movement—all of which have made it increasingly clear to leaders within the conservative movement and within the Republican Party that their uneasy association with the Birch Society must be terminated.

But during the past year, the Birch Society has enjoyed a period of considerable expansion.

In addition to the home office in Belmont, Mass., and branch offices in Brookfield, Massachusetts, and San Marino, California, new offices have been opened in White Plains, New York, Glenview, Illinois, Newport Beach, California, Dallas, Texas, and Washington, D.C., and additional offices have been opened in Belmont, Massachusetts. Many of these new offices are fairly small operations, but the administrative and office staffs would now number considerably more than the sixty that were required a year ago.

The field staff of full-time coordinators has been expanded from forty to seventy according to the *Bulletin* for July, 1965.

In the November, 1965, *Bulletin,* it is reported that there has also been a substantial increase in the gross income of the Society —from $3,200,000 for 1964 to an estimated $5,200,000 for 1965. Part of this increase would certainly come from the dues of new members, but a substantial portion comes from the greatly increased sale of literature—the sales pitches for which occupy the major portion of every monthly *Bulletin.*

Published estimates of the current membership of the Society range from 60,000 to 100,000. And the Birch Society leadership quotes these estimates with approval. There is reason, however, to view this estimate with caution. The number of letters actually written by Birch Society members in response to strongly suggested items on the Agenda of the monthly *Bulletins* has always been far below this figure.

A prime case in point was the letter-writing campaign that

tried unsuccessfully to discourage the Xerox Corporation from producing a series of television shows on the work of the United Nations. This campaign was launched in the *Bulletin* for June, 1964, and the Birch Society concentrated on it in *Bulletins* for the next eight months. The Xerox Corporation did not assume that all of the 51,279 letters of protest that it received were from any one group, but because of the flood of mail, it did assign a staff to catalogue the letters. The staff found that many individuals had written several times and that the total of 51,279 protesting letters received represented only 12,785 individuals.[20]

Gordon Hall, the lecturer on extremist groups on both the left and the right, estimates the current membership to be no more than 27,000.[21] He bases this figure on a number of Birch Society letter-writing campaigns such as the one to the Xerox Corporation. Another index to which he points is the paid circulation of *American Opinion*. There is a constant item in the *Bulletins* urging subscriptions to *American Opinion* for members and their friends and the total paid circulation in 1965 averaged 35,400, according to the December, 1965, issue.

Mr. Hall comments also that the Society simply is not able to get out the crowds for picketing and demonstrations in the way the extremist left seems able to do.

A curious curtain of secrecy is also reported by Mr. Hall between individual chapters in any given area. Members have frequently told him that, while their particular chapter doesn't have many members or do very much, "all the other chapters are very strong." Mr. Hall says he hears this same thing from members of "strong" chapters with whom he talks and his speaking engagements take him all over the country.

Gordon Hall also reports that recruitment into Birch Society chapters seems to go very slowly. Often, he says, people can be persuaded to attend one or two meetings, but then they just never show up again.

Mr. Hall also has some doubts about the membership estimates because Robert Welch, who has always before refused to make any statement about total membership, has taken to using the public estimate of 60,000–100,000 members and quotes it happily. Further, when Mr. Hall recently asked John Rousselot, the number two man in the Birch Society hierarchy who now serves as their "National Director of Public Relations," about the total membership, Mr. Rousselot said "I don't know," and then added, "probably 60,000–100,000." But Mr. Rousselot refused a friendly wager with Mr. Hall on the accuracy of this estimate.

What, then, is the membership of the John Birch Society? It may be that there are actually 60,000 or 75,000 or 100,000 people who have joined the Birch Society at one time or another. But all the evidence related to *active* membership suggests a smaller figure, probably between 25,000 and 30,000.

Whither the John Birch Society?

As the full weight of the Goldwater defeat has sunk home in the minds of the leaders and members of the conservative movement and of the Republican Party, and as the divisive role played by the members of the John Birch Society has become clearer to all, it has become more and more difficult for the Birch Society to find people who are receptive to their myopic ideological line. Further, many of those persons who comprised the influx of membership following Goldwater's defeat are rabidly anti-Negro.

I will be quite surprised if the Birch Society manages to reach any significant number of new members in the wake of its widespread repudiation. If they are able to maintain the flow of income of from fifteen to twenty thousand dollars a day which they need for their current level of operation, they will be able to retain the large field staff of organizers and coordinators which they must have to recruit new members and to maintain even a semblance of order in the chapter organizations.

One of the things that may help to underwrite the expenses of this essential field staff is the considerable shift in emphasis that has been made toward greater and greater reliance upon the sale of literature. The lengthy *Bulletin* for November, 1965, which is to serve as the "operating manual" for the Society for the next several months, has page after page of books, packets, pamphlets, and stickers for sale. One of the more extraordinary items offered is a long-playing set of records (18 hours) entitled *One Dozen Trumpets*—a set of recordings of a *three-day* marathon speech by no other than The Founder. It can be yours for only fifty dollars!

This shift to the sale of literature and of other various and sundry audio and visual aids in the battle against "the international Communist conspiracy" has skewed the income of the Society so that now, according to Robert Welch, membership dues cover only about one-third of the total costs.[22] But the "hard sell" on literature may be the thing that keeps the Society afloat.

If income is maintained at a level high enough to keep a substantial number of coordinators in the field, the John Birch Society will be able to retain at least a semblance of life.

The members of the Council of the Society still have a great stake in maintaining the "respectability" of an organization to which they have lent the prestige of their names. The "organization men" also have a stake in the maintenance and enhancement of the "respectability" of the John Birch Society. But shut off by the repudiation of conservative and Republican Party leaders from the most natural sources of membership, recruiting will have to move more and more toward those on the social, political, and psychological "fringes" of our society. Thus profound strains are bound to develop between its desired image of "respectability" and a possible further shift toward the attitudes of the racist fringe now within its membership. With organizers out there in the field, they can always find fifteen or twenty persons in any given locality who, if given enough personal attention and encouragement, could be signed up for almost anything. The image of respectability may become increasingly difficult to maintain—even in the eyes of its leaders and members.

Since the John Birch Society is made up of fellow citizens, and since the Society is apt to be with us—perhaps in even more virulent forms—for some time to come, it is important for us to deal with it in ways that strengthen rather than weaken the integrity of our democratic processes.

The terrible assassination of President Kennedy brought home to all thoughtful people our laxity in allowing the creation of an atmosphere of hate, and fear, and suspicion in which assassination was not only possible, but almost expected.

Therefore, it would seem to me that our first task, if we are to be responsible citizens, is to clear our country of this atmosphere of blind hate, of unreasoning fear, and of incredibly gullible suspicion from whatever source. I suppose that men must still have the freedom to rise and say that Chief Justice Warren is an agent of the Communists and should be impeached, that we would be as well represented in the UN if we had traded Adlai Stevenson for Andrei Gromyko, that Martin Luther King is a Communist. Men will still rise to say such things, but it is clearer now that we have the responsibility to rise, in turn, and challenge them. They have a right to speak. We have a responsibility to identify them for what they are. As responsible citizens we ought no longer to let inflammatory charges go unchallenged.

But members of the Birch Society do not spend all their time making accusations against persons. Some of them touch upon real issues and problems in many areas of our national life. But the most that can be said for the great majority of the members and leaders is that "where they are scratching there is an itch"—but their insistent scratching is only broadening the inflammation.

One would ordinarily expect to look at the ideology and activity of a movement of social protest to identify the fundamental issues in conflict. But as we have seen, this particular movement of social protest has moved deep within the categories of irrationality. This is you will recall also characteristic of its mode of conflict—a style of irrational conflict that is highly acrimonious, propagandistic—with no attempt to resolve issues, which broadens rather than narrows, and which is resolved only as it falls of its own weight.

Because of this irrational style of conflict the followers of Welch provide no means for the correction of the irrationalities of their ideology. They see any who challenge their beliefs as an enemy to be destroyed. Opposition is error, for they "know" that they have the truth.

Because of these two inextricably bound reasons: an irrational ideology, and an irrational style of conflict, the John Birch Society and its leaders have made no positive contribution to our national life. Their influence since the founding in late 1958 has, in fact, been unrelievedly negative. Professing to "alert" Americans, they have succeeded only in creating fear and hatred of a grotesque caricature of the Communist menace that exists not in fact, but only in their imaginations. Professing to "inform" Americans, they have succeeded in some localities in helping to create an atmosphere of suspicion and hate in which libel is standard and violence expected. Professing to "defend" our nation from itself, they have had an influential role in defining any action on such issues as disarmament and integration as "Un-American" or "Unconstitutional." But most inexcusably, they have clouded the arenas of conflict. Their irrational, closed-minded ideology and their irrational style of conflict have made it extremely difficult openly and publicly to clarify and consider matters of grave import to our country during this era of crisis. Rather than join in the clarification and consideration of real alternatives to real problems, they have chosen to escape and to propose simple-minded and foolhardy alternatives for dealing with the only problem they seem able to acknowledge. If the members of the Birch Society and their leaders want to escape from the hard choices of the real world, that's their business, but "escape" becomes our business when most of their efforts serve only to prevent clarification and public discussion of the real problems by the rest of us.

Co-Existence at Home

As we view the irrational conflict and ideology of the Birch Society, most people would agree that our democracy is better served when its decision-making processes are more nearly channeled within the bounds of rationality. How then may opponents of the Birch Society not only co-exist, but perhaps even move toward potentially constructive rational debate and conflict?

First of all, opponents of the Birch Society should have enough trust in rational democratic processes to abide by their norms. Of course all opponents of the Birch Society will not be willing to do this or to grant the right of any and all to be heard

within the political arena. But the core of local Birch Society opposition must be willing to attack allies as loudly and clearly as
they do the Birch Society for any abandonment of the norms of
rational conflict.

Second, opponents should respond to a specific major charge
early in a conflict with the Birch Society and stop right there.
Ignoring the build-up of further propagandistic charges, opponents should refuse to discuss any of them until local members or
leaders of the Society have come to rational debate upon that
specific one. If such debate is refused or avoided, opponents
should protest this fact persistently and loudly until the public
either loses interest because of the lack of "progress" of the conflict
or until the public itself "reads the Society out" of the rationally
legitimate arena of conflict. Once having selected such a charge or
issue, opponents of the Society should *never* abandon contention
over it unless they are, in fact, bested in rational debate. If no
other resolution of the conflict over this specific initial charge
comes, opponents should always protest the fact that representatives of the Birch Society refused to engage in rational debate over
it. There have been a number of more or less successful attempts
at this kind of debate with the Birch Society. Some representatives
of the Massachusetts Council of Churches offered to discuss with
Welch the most effective ways of combatting communism. When
this offer was ignored by Welch, there was, unfortunately, little
protest raised by the Massachusetts Council of Churches over
Welch's refusal to enter into such a reasonable discussion.

In Boston there was a less polite challenge issued to Welch
to defend his attack upon UNICEF Christmas greeting cards in
a public debate. His failure to respond was somewhat more widely
publicized.

But Welch's characterization of Eisenhower as "a conscious
agent of the Communist conspiracy" and the continual requests
for explanation or apology by opponents of Welch provides a
prime example of such tenacious handling of an issue. This charge
is one that understandably embarrasses many of Welch's followers. The opponents of the Society have continually asked for further comment on the charge. But to date, Welch has given noth-

ing that would begin to approach a satisfactory explanation of the charge for either his opponents or for the general public.

Third, opponents should also insist that local members and leaders of the Birch Society themselves observe norms of rational conflict. They should point out to representatives of the Society and to the uncommitted public when and how these norms are violated by the followers of Welch. Though not involving the Birch Society, an excellent example of such an insistence upon rational conflict is provided in the following:

> In a recent controversy in Cincinnati over the left-wing political history of the city planning director, supporters of the director and of the councilman who hired him formed a "Committee of 150 for Political Morality." This Committee used considerable sophistication in the selection of a name and in their whole campaign. Rather than remain on the defensive, and let the opposition blanket the community with charges of subversion, this committee invoked an equally strong value—of morality in politics—and took the offensive against the use of personal attack by their opponents. This technique constitutes a way in which controversy can be held on a relatively high plane: by invoking community norms against smears, using these very norms as an issue of the controversy.[23]

Finally, whenever it may become appropriate and necessary, it is to be remembered by opponents of the Birch Society that the courts provide legal recourse against libel and slander.

Thus the norms of rational political conflict may be upheld and strengthened by the fidelity of opponents of the Society to them. They may be demonstrated by insistence upon early debate on a particular charge or issue. And they may be enforced through insistence upon them to the Birch Society, before the public, and through the courts. Only as members and leaders of the Society are compelled to engage in rational political conflict is there any possibility that they might exert a constructive influence within our nation.

It is sobering to remind ourselves and to remind even the Birchers that, if we do not defend freedom and rationality as the norms of political conflict, we ought not to be surprised to find ourselves caught in a totalitarianism not only from the left or from the right, but perhaps even from the center.

Notes

CHAPTER I

1. Robert Welch, *The Politician* (Belmont: Robert Welch, 1963). The year 1963 is the date when *The Politician* was made public by Welch. Up until that time copies were circulated by Welch. *The Politician* has also been labeled "The Black Book" (partly) because of the color of its cardboard cover. *The Blue Book* was also so named (partly) because of the color of its cover.
2. Robert Welch, *The Blue Book of the John Birch Society.*
3. Associated Press story in the *Christian Science Monitor,* April 1, 1961.
4. *The Politician,* p. 278.
5. *The Politician,* pp. 276-277.
6. *See* Welch's "Prologue" to *The Politician,* pp. ix-xi.
7. *Ibid.,* p. xiii.
8. *Ibid.,* p. xi.
9. The Boston *Globe,* April 1, 1961.
10. *The Politician,* pp. xii-xiii.
11. Welch, *Blue Book,* p. 29.
12. This "paraphrase" of Lenin is in the *Blue Book,* pp. 10-11.
13. *Ibid.,* pp. 11-12.
14. *Ibid.,* p. 39.
15. *Ibid.*
16. *Ibid.,* p. 45.
17. *Ibid.,* p. 63.
18. *Ibid.,* pp. 65-66.
19. *Ibid.,* pp. 75-76.
20. *Ibid.,* p. 86.
21. *Ibid.,* p. 94.
22. *Ibid.,* p. 96.
23. *Ibid.,* p. 97.
24. *Ibid.,* p. 112.
25. *Ibid.,* p. 126.
26. *Ibid.,* p. 136.
27. *Ibid.,* p. 138.
28. *Ibid.,* p. 141.
29. *Ibid.,* pp. 149-150. It is very revealing that Welch fails to include the fourth question of any theology—the relationship between man and man. But issues of ethics are a blind spot for any who, like Welch and Goldwater, carry individualism to its logical, egocentric, and self-destructive extreme.
30. *Ibid.,* p. 153.

31. *Ibid.*, p. 159.
32. *Ibid.*, p. 162.
33. *Ibid.*, p. 158.

CHAPTER II

1. Robert H. W. Welch, Jr., *The Life of John Birch* (Chicago: Henry Regnery Company, 1954).
2. C. R. Daley, "The John Birch I Knew," *Western Recorder*, General Association of Baptists in Kentucky, April 13, 1961, pp. 4-5.
3. Welch, *The Life of John Birch*, title page.
4. From "The Ballad of John Birch" by Douglas Morse, a portion of which appears in *American Opinion*, Feb., 1964, p. 96.
5. This biographical material is drawn from an appendix appearing in the second printing of the *Blue Book*, and from interviews with observers within the business and political communities of Boston.
6. Welch, *Blue Book*, p. 62.
7. See Welch, *Blue Book*, pp. 63 and 150, for example.
8. For example Welch sees religion as instrumental to the morality of the Western world and sees its demise as leading to the rise of "amoral man." Welch, *Blue Book*, pp. 62-66. Compare this with Spengler's view.
9. Welch, *Blue Book*, p. 116.
10. *Ibid.*, pp. 113-114.
11. *Ibid.*, p. 119.
12. *Bulletin*, March, 1962, p. 10.
13. Boston *Herald*, Sept. 16, 1956.
14. *Bulletin*, July, 1963, p. 1.
15. *Ibid.*, June, 1960, pp. 24-28.
16. See the issue of *American Opinion* for July, August, and September of 1960 entitled, "A World Gone Crazy; a Panoramic survey of the degree of Communist influence in each of 107 countries."
17. Welch, *Blue Book*, p. 116.
18. *Ibid.*
19. *Ibid.*, p. 142.
20. *Ibid.*, pp. 113-26.
21. *Ibid.*, p. 109.
22. *Ibid.*, p. 159.
23. *Ibid.*, p. 119.
24. *Ibid.*, p. 122.
25. *Ibid.*, p. 123.
26. *Ibid.*, p. 121.
27. *Ibid.*, p. 125.
28. *Ibid.*, p. 5.
29. *Ibid.*

CHAPTER III

1. From a report by Jerome Sullivan in the evening Boston *Globe* of March 29, 1961.
2. Welch, *Blue Book*, pp. 163-164.
3. *Ibid.*, p. 164-165.
4. *Ibid.*, p. 165.

5. *Ibid.,* p. 165-166.
6. *Ibid.,* p. 159, underlining added.
7. *Ibid.,* appendix.
8. Most of my interviews with these men were in the spring of 1962.
9. See the pamphlet written and published by Koch entitled "A Business Man Looks at Communism."

CHAPTER IV
1. Most of my interviews with these men were in the spring of 1962. Some of them have been given fictional names.
2. Los Angeles *Herald and Express,* August 25, 1961.
3. A UPI story in the Boston *Traveler,* April 11, 1961.
4. April 23, 1961.

CHAPTER V
1. Most of the interviews reported in this chapter were conducted during the spring of 1962. Many of the names are fictional.
2. This report of Bud Lanker was published in a series of four articles in the Arizona *Journal,* May 1-4, 1962.
3. The Los Angeles *Times,* March 12, 1961.
4. Welch, *Blue Book,* p. 170.
5. *Ibid.,* p. 158.

CHAPTER VI
1. The statement of the ideological beliefs of the John Birch Society in these next two chapters is drawn from personal interviews with the members and leaders of the Birch Society. In the course of most of these interviews I also used a questionnaire which was designed primarily to discover whether ideological beliefs were held in an open-minded or a closed-minded way. I have drawn upon the publications of the Society at points where they illustrate or illuminate a particular ideological belief. But *no* organization is so "monolithic" that you can describe the thoughts of its leaders and members simply by reading its official literature.
2. Welch, *Blue Book,* pp. 129-136.
3. Welch, *Blue Book,* footnote 14 following page 112. In this footnote, Welch identifies C.A.S.E. as one of the most successful national fronts to date.
4. Welch, *Bulletin,* Dec., 1961, p. 8.
5. *Ibid.,* Feb., 1960, insert.
6. *Ibid.,* May, 1960, p. 22.
7. New York *Times,* Nov. 12, 1961.
8. The New York *Times Magazine,* Oct. 1, 1961, p. 96.
9. Welch, *Bulletin,* Sept. 1961, p. 10.
10. *Ibid.,* Jan., 1962, p. 16.
11. The AAUN welcomes letters or visitors asking questions or requesting information on any aspect of the operations of the UN. The quotations are drawn from several "Facts" pamphlets and from a more extended eighty-page statement of "Questions and Answers on the United Nations" written by Arthur Larson. All this material is available through the American Association for the United Nations, 345 East 46th Street, New York 17, New York.

12. I would add a third possible explanation: that an internal conspiracy of such vast proportions does not, in fact, exist.
13. Welch, *American Opinion*, July, August, and September, 1960 (combined issue) , center section.
14. This incident was carried by UPI and reported in the Portland, Maine *Press Herald*, Feb. 14, 1963.
15. Welch, *Bulletin*, Jan., 1963, p. 30.

CHAPTER VII

1. Compare this view with that of Martin E. Marty, "Mr. Welch's Messianic Consciousness; A Review of the John Birch Society's *Blue Book*," *The Christian Century*, May 31, 1961, pp. 683-684.
2. This study is available through either the Division of World Missions or the Board of Christian Social Concerns of The Methodist Church.
3. Shreveport, La.: The Drake Company, 1961.
4. Welch, *Blue Book*, p. 59.
5. *Ibid.*
6. This speech was reported in the *Christian Science Monitor*, April 18, 1961.
7. See "On the Differences Between a Democracy and a Republic" widely distributed as a separate pamphlet, but also included in the Appendix of *The White Book of The John Birch Society for 1961*.
8. This observation by Schwartz was reported by Cabell Phillips, the New York *Times*, April 30, 1961.

CHAPTER VIII

1. Welch, *Blue Book*, p. 43.
2. The members and leaders of the Birch Society to whom a questionnaire was administered were high on general authoritarianism, very high on general intolerance, and therefore high in the more inclusive concept of dog-matic closed-mindedness of which the foregoing are components. The con-cept of the open and closed mind and the Dogmatism and Opinionation Scales by which it is quantified were used in my questionnaire and are drawn from the research of Milton Rokeach as reported in *The Open and Closed Mind*, New York: Basic Books, Inc., 1960.
3. *Ibid.*, p. 70.
4. For an excellent discussion of anomie see Robert K. Merton, *Social Theory and Social Structure* (Rev. ed. Glencoe, Ill.: The Free Press, 1959) , pp. 131-95.
5. See Daniel Bell's analysis of the displacement of the older military, business, and social elites by the growing power and status of the emerging technical, theoretical, and scientific intellectual elites—particularly in business and in governmental, military, and economic decision-making. Daniel Bell, "The Dispossessed—1962," in the book edited by him entitled *The Radical Right* (Garden City, N.Y.: Doubleday & Company, Inc., 1963) , pp. 1-38.
6. See the discussion of these strains in the excellent article by Talcott Par-sons entitled "Age and Sex in the Social Structure of the United States." Clyde Kluckhohn and Henry Murray (eds.) , *Personality in Nature Society and Culture* (Second ed. N.Y.: Alfred A. Knopf, 1959) , pp. 363-75.
7. See the discussion of the mechanism of frustration-aggression in Gordon W. Allport, *The Nature of Prejudice* (Abridged. Garden City, N.Y.: Dou-

bleday Anchor Books, Doubleday & Company, Inc., 1958) . Chapters 21 and 22.
8. *Ibid.,* p. 331.

CHAPTER IX

1. *American Opinion,* July-August, 1965, p. 70.
2. See *Ibid.,* pp. 70, 74, 77-80.
3. *Ibid.,* p. 78.
4. *Ibid.,* p. 78.
5. *Ibid.,* p. 75.
6. *Ibid.,* pp. 76-77.
7. *Ibid.,* p. 81.
8. *Ibid.,* p. 80.
9. *National Review,* Oct. 19, 1965, p. 917.
10. A UPI story, Washington, printed in the Bangor, Maine, *Daily News,* Sept. 30, 1965.
11. Associated Press story, printed in the Portland, Maine, *Press Herald,* Oct. 1, 1965.
12. Welch, *Bulletin,* Nov., 1965, p. 122.
13. *Ibid.*
14. Issue dated Sept. 7, 1965.
15. See *Time,* March 20, 1964.
16. Welch, *Bulletin,* August, 1965, pp. 18-20.
17. *Ibid.,* Nov., 1965, p. 61.
18. *Ibid.,* pp. 69-70.
19. *Ibid.,* p. 135.
20. *New York Times,* March 7, 1965.
21. This material was provided by Mr. Hall on November 10, 1965.
22. Welch, *Bulletin* for November, 1965, p. 74.
23. James S. Coleman, *Community Conflict* (Glencoe, Ill.: The Free Press, 1957), p. 12.

Index

27